"Donna Greene is a woman of compassion and spiritual depth. Because she has led Community Ministry for Girls for more than 25 years, thousands of girls have learned how the Bible meets precisely their everyday needs. To God be the glory for the laying down of her life for those hungry young women! I love her statement: 'The key is relationship. The Word of God and the souls of men are the only two things that will last forever.'

"Donna has been through the mill of suffering with breast cancer, but has come forth as gold. She is eminently qualified to teach, able to sympathize, and her heart overflows with love for her girls. I know—I have watched them."

—*Elisabeth Elliot*

Growing Godly Women

GROWING GODLY WOMEN

A Christian Woman's Guide
to Mentoring Teenage Girls

Donna Margaret Greene

New Hope Publishers
Birmingham, Alabama

New Hope Publishers
P. O. Box 12065
Birmingham, AL 35202-2065
www.newhopepubl.com

Library of Congress Cataloging-in-Publication Data
Greene, Donna Margaret, 1947-
Growing Godly women : a Christian woman's guide to mentoring teenage girls / Donna Margaret Greene.
p. cm.
ISBN 1-56309-744-3
1.   Teenage girls-Religious life. 2. Teenage girls-Conduct of life.
3.   Mothers and daughters. 4. Parenting-Religious aspects-Christianity. I. Title.
BV4551.3 .G74 2003
259'.23--dc21
2002013017

Cover design by Righteous Planet Design Studio

ISBN: 1-56309-744-3
N034107•0103•10M1

Dedication

"Train a child in the way he should go, and when he is old he will not turn from it" (Prov. 22:6).

With love and appreciation to my parents, Sara Sugg Greene (Williams) and Joseph Francis Greene; and my southern grandparents, Lillian Belle Williams Sugg and Gholston Thomas Sugg, who dedicated me to the Lord before I was born, taught me the truths of the Scriptures, took me to church every time the doors opened, and prayed that I would grow up and go into full-time Christian work.

With love and appreciation to my youth director, Nancy James Sayers, who invested in my life so sacrificially at such a crucial time, who gave me a vision for ministry, and who taught me how to serve.

With love and appreciation to Barbara and Frank Barker. For Frank's vision and wisdom to allow me the freedom to create whatever ministry God had in mind, without limitations. For Barbara's and Frank's lives, which taught me never to underestimate the power and faithfulness of God.

With love and appreciation for Birmingham Theological Seminary and all the professors who taught me well. The very first verse on my very first test was "Should you then seek great things for yourself? Seek them not" (Jer. 45:5). With thankfulness for a seminary which teaches the Bible as God's infallible word and makes it practical in everyday life. May all I learned, the notes I took and saved be used for the glory of God.

With extra love and appreciation for those very first Bible study girls. We shared it all. You will always be the "originals." Thank you for what you've become. You've lived well above the level of mediocrity and have soared as eagles in life. You're an inspiration to me.

It all began with Frank Barker saying, "Why don't you let the church pay you this summer?" and my reply, "For what?"

"It doesn't matter," he said. "Whatever you dream up. You have a remarkable gift with children." His daughter, Anita, then 11 years old, went to her knees and begged, "Oh, please, please, please! Start a club for me and my friends."

Thus a ministry was born.

To God be the glory! Great things He has done.

Contents

Introduction 3

1: Creating the Ties That Bind 19

2: What Makes Girls Tick, and What Ticks Them Off 29

3: Mentor, Leader, Friend 37

4: The Word, the Mentor, and Relationships 49

5: The Bible and Today's Girls 59

6: Lessons in Love, Grace, and Beauty 69

7: Lessons in Serving Others 85

8: Girls, Groups, Identity, and Belonging 93

9: The Importance of Rewards 105

10: Developing Effective Bible Studies 111

11: Using Stories to Teach 121

12: Teaching Through Activities 131

Reflections 141

Afterword 149

Appendix 155

Acknowledgments

God uses many people to influence our lives. In reflecting upon Community Ministry for Girls, I am aware that it would not be what it has become today without the love, support, and encouragement of countless hundreds of faithful, interested friends.

A tremendous thank-you to the numerous families who have opened their homes to the girls for weekly meetings and parties; to those who have provided thousands of drinks and cookies; and to those who have prepared, poured, and cleaned up. To those who have shared their beach houses and condos, big-city apartments, lake houses, farms, mountain homes, vehicles, boats, and swimming pools, you have provided places and opportunities for God to change lives and for girls to establish bonds. A special thank-you to the hundreds of individuals who have supported this ministry financially and to Briarwood Presbyterian Church and Covenant Presbyterian Church, both of which have gone above and beyond in their sacrificial giving and encouragement.

Thank you to the following people who have contributed to this book: Britt Adams, Kate Adams, Anita Barker Barnes, Leila Welch Brazeal, Carol Colquitt Godwin, Melissa Craig, Charlotte Gage, Lynn Haskew Graham, Rebecca Hiller, Katherine Jackson, Beth Huff Jordan, Tracy Wheeler Jones, Lacy Kerr, Shelby Kerr, Elizabeth Klyce, Sarah Katherine Lever, Ellen Magnus, Frannie Major, Maggie McDonald, Leta McGehee, Holly Harrison Moore, Emily Snuggs Neel, Louise Parsons, Carrie

Pittman, Julie Preston, Amanda Pridgen, Allison Riley, Carol Harris Riley, Shalonne Sevier, Dr. Milner Snuggs, Kate Stutts, Brantley Townsend, Jeanne Upchurch, Melanie Beard Walker, and Wendy Wooden.

Thank you to Sharon Head, the administrative assistant for Community Ministry for Girls, who put all these words into the computer and returned them to me in manuscript form. Without her help, this book may never have come to be.

Introduction

Introduction

*Is there anything of which one can say,
"Look! This is something new"?
It was here already, long ago;
it was here before our time.
(Eccl. 1:10)*

Though times change, some things remain the same. Ultimately there is nothing new under the sun. While our world is different in many ways from the Old Testament writer's world, and the girls in today's Community Ministry for Girls are in some ways different from those first-generation girls, basic human needs transcend time.

Ours is a society filled with comfort and modern technology, though many people in the world still live in untold suffering and poverty. We live in an instant society. We pop dinner in the microwave directly from the freezer and it's ready in a few minutes. We get upset at fast-food restaurants if we have to wait too long for our orders to be taken or filled. Machines wash our clothes and dishes. Automobiles, airplanes, and trains take us directly and quickly to our desired destinations.

Computers process our thoughts and link us throughout the globe. Although wires and satellites connect us, ours is still a very lonely, isolated society. While the Internet in some ways unites us, in so many cases we are disconnected at the heart. The fast pace of our days denies us the basic need and privilege of communication at its deepest levels. We hurry from one activity to another. Rarely do we stop and just be still, listen, or think; though without these times of reflection and evaluation we can easily lose and perhaps never find our true selves.

Ours is a media-saturated culture. Adolescent girls in particular are told how to dress, what to think, and how to act in both very blatant and subtle ways. Mixed messages constantly bombard the minds of girls. "Be beautiful," they hear on the one hand. "Beauty is only skin deep," another voice tells them. Magazines and commercials place tremendous emphasis upon makeup, fashion, hair, and weight. They rarely mention anorexia, bulimia, and multiple eating disorders that may arise from trying to become too thin or too perfect. Rarer still do they speak of inner qualities such as character, beliefs, values, attitudes, and talents.

We all, but adolescent girls in particular, live in a much more dangerous world with less protection than our mothers and grandmothers. Consider the following statistics.*

TOP OFFENSES IN PUBLIC SCHOOLS

1940	1982	1996–97
1. Talking	1. Rape	1. Attacks/fights without weapon
2. Gum chewing	2. Robbery	2. Theft
3. Making noise	3. Assault	3. Vandalism
4. Running in halls	4. Burglary	4. Attacks/fights with weapon
5. Getting out of turn in line	5. Arson	5. Robbery
6. Wearing improper clothing	6. Bombings	6. Rape

Not only have American families drastically changed throughout the last several decades, they are literally under siege. Parents are more likely to be overworked, overcommitted, tired, and poor. Often they receive minimal outside support. Many parents have little time to devote to proper supervision and encouragement of their children. Children in turn can easily become lost in the shuffle or even distance themselves from families.

Our society has gone crazy over sex! Advertisements, movies, songs, and television shows place tremendous emphasis on sexuality, being sexy, and sexual drives. Sexual pressure, sexual violence, casual sex—all are a part of our daily lives, particularly the lives of adolescents.

Perhaps the greatest pressure adolescent girls face comes directly from their peers. Peer pressure encourages or forces people to follow the standards, conduct, way of thinking, and values of those around them. This pressure can be either good or bad, depending upon the value system of the group. Peer pressure constantly tells us what we think of ourselves, what we think of others, what is right and wrong, what to wear, and how to act. Hardly anything seems to influence us as much as the opinions of the people we spend time with every day.

Adolescence is marked by an intense preoccupation with self, which grows and changes daily. Puberty is the biological process of that change, but adolescence is a personal experience of that process. In adolescence, girls often experience tremendous social pressure to deny who they really are. Comparison to others is rampant. Academic pressure is constant and much of life is a consistent drama of competition. Most girls display only a small portion of their gifts and talents. Everything about adolescent girls is changing—body shape, hormones, skin, attitudes, and feelings. Questions constantly arise: What is the meaning of my life? Where do I fit in? What is my place in this world? In the midst of this constant change, girls are likely evaluated first and foremost by appearance. Each girl must learn to accept her own body and looks and become the person she really is.

Teenage girls need a place where they feel safe and have the freedom to move about independently—a place to grow and develop into their own uniqueness. Their moods are often intense, changeable, and uncommunicative. Small events can trigger enormous reactions. They deal with reality, despair, and anger in various ways. Loving adults who care and are concerned can play a big part in their lives. In order to become strong, a girl must connect to emotions and work through them. The emotional reasoning of an adolescent is "if you feel something is true, it must be true."

Adolescents tend to see things in black and white. They are absolute in their judgments and have trouble putting events and thoughts into perspective. A mature adult can listen for what a girl says, as well as what she is not saying. While the outward appearance is often one of awkwardness, energy, restlessness, moodiness, and anger, deep within is the struggle to find oneself—an attempt to find a place to fit in. Everyone wants to be accepted, to fit in, to be popular. Any way we look at it, there's a price to be paid. Everyone lives with the pain of discipline or the pain of regret. With adolescents, surface behavior tries to convey little of the struggle within.

Adolescent girls need to learn to deal with feelings honestly. If a girl does not have the freedom to express her feelings, if her anger is not tolerated and love is withheld from her when anger is displayed, the girl is unable to grow into the person she can become. She denies her true self for the approval of others. Eventually, she will stop expressing unacceptable feelings. Unacceptable behavior will cease, at least in front of adults. She will no longer reveal deep secrets and thoughts and turn inward.

This results in any number of problems. Depression comes if a girl places blame on herself for failure or inability to live up to the standards of others. Anger erupts if she places the blame on others such as parents, peers, or culture. Once she can express negative feelings, her capacity for joy is recovered. If she cannot express her anger, she may turn to drugs, alcohol, or other addictions to help closet the pain.

Though adolescent girls constantly face new challenges and obstacles, they share basic needs common to everyone. They need loving people who will talk to them and support them as they journey through the many ups and downs of their teenage years. They need supervision. They need help in getting organized and reaching toward and completing goals. Encouragement is absolutely necessary for a young girl to have the ability to grow into a productive adult. When caring adults take the time to teach values and share information, girls can make a healthy transition from adolescence to adulthood. Once girls understand the influence and effect of society and culture in their lives, they can fight back. They can make wise choices. They can decide for themselves what their values will be and set standards for themselves.

The more a girl knows herself and what she believes, the less the pressure her peers apply can control her. She can determine to make a difference and not just blend. A mentor, teacher, youth leader, or older friend who steps in at this most crucial point of life and becomes an encourager or guide can make all the difference in an adolescent girl's life. A mentor is someone farther down the road, going in the direction these young girls want and need to go. A mentor shares her own gifts and wisdom in order to help another person get there.

From the time I became a Christian at the age of 9, I knew deep down inside that God was calling me into full-time Christian work. As a child, my concern was that He would send me to Africa, a place far away and unknown. Now, as an adult, I know that His plan for me was to become a Bible teacher in my own community.

While the prospect of going overseas did not seem right for me, the love of children and working with children has always been there. God has a way of taking our gifts, talents, and interests and using them to do the work He has planned for us. The wonderful plan He had for me would turn out to be one that not only suited me but one that would get better and better as the years went by.

I was a flight attendant (then called stewardess) for 2 years with a major American airline, a job I took right out of college. Then I decided that it was time for me to start "changing the world." With a major in psychology and sociology, I wanted to do social work with children—maybe even work for or start an orphanage. It did not take long for me to see that my plans were shifting and God's plans were forming.

For a time I worked with Head Start, a program for underprivileged preschool children. The following summer, Rev. Frank Barker suggested that I work for Briarwood Presbyterian Church. When I asked him what he wanted me to do, he replied, "Whatever you think up. You have a remarkable gift with children." His daughter, Anita, then 11 years old, immediately spoke up. "Please start a club for me and my friends." Community Ministry for Girls was born.

Twelve girls representing four schools attended the first meeting. Through the subsequent years, over 3,000 girls representing at least 30 different schools have been a part of this Bible study ministry. The group has always been interdenominational, focusing on pulling girls in from schools rather than churches. One year we did a tally and found that out of approximately 400 girls there were 43 different churches represented from nine different denominations. Presently, a girl can become a member of Community Ministry for Girls when she begins the fifth grade and can be a part of it until she graduates from high school. Grades 5 through 9 meet in the afternoons and the high school girls come at night.

The ministry is based on Luke 2:52, "And Jesus increased in wisdom and stature, and in favor with God and man." The ministry's emphasis is on the girls' mental, physical, spiritual, and social growth. Along with weekly Bible studies and Scripture memory, girls participate in service projects in the community as well as parties, weekend retreats, and trips. The ministry is designed to train a girl to be a balanced Christian—to take in and give out at the same time.

A girl's first Bible-based lessons begin with cliques and how to deal with and break them. Reaching out, getting to know new people, and making everyone feel welcome is a big part of the ministry. If a girl does not feel comfortable, she will not want to come back. We emphasize this from the time a girl begins until she leaves the group to go to college. Hopefully this mind-set will follow her throughout her life.

From teachings on cliques, the girls go on to study books of the Bible, as well as many topics that are pertinent to their everyday lives. So much of life is caught rather than taught. It is important that they learn lessons that will make a difference in their day-to-day living. As the girls grow and learn together, they gradually form a peer group that will support and help them as they face all the pressures that bombard adolescents today.

Community Ministry for Girls conveys a feeling of sisterhood, camaraderie, and friendship. Girls wear our logo on T-shirts, sweatshirts, jackets, hats, shorts, nightshirts, and other items like binders and pens that they bring to the weekly meetings. Everyone is always welcome to attend, and anyone can wear the logo. We desire that no one feels left out. This form of identification and practice also helps in the everyday life at school.

Leadership is another quality we highly stress. Role models are so important in an adolescent's life. Older girls in the ministry become leaders of the younger girls. After each Bible study, the fifth- and sixth-grade girls break up into small groups a high school girl leads. She is able to be their friend and give personal attention to each of them. College-aged girls help give leadership to the older girls. The ministry lends itself to develop leaders from within. At a very early age, these girls learn responsibility and leadership skills.

We reap what we sow, but often we reap much later than we sow. It takes an average of 2 years to really get to know a young person. The average youth worker gives up after about 18 months. Almost 30 years in this ministry have given me a clearer perspective as I look back on those years.

"Train a child in the way he should go, and when he is old he will not turn from it" (Prov. 22:6).

Community Ministry for Girls is now in its second generation. The daughter of one of the original girls is now in her seventh year of the ministry. Many alumnae have moved out of town, married, and started groups for their daughters and their friends. Countless girls have gone to college and have immediately begun to lead groups and share with others what they have learned. The logo has become a symbol that helps girls recognize their sisters, from the youngest girls in the ministry to those who are now grown.

I did not come into this with a plan for what the ministry would be or what it would become. When women from other cities ask me how to begin a program like this, I quickly respond, "The key is relationship." The Bible study element of the ministry turns the investment of God's Word into a personal, practical, real relationship with the Lord Jesus Christ—which in turn spills over into every other relationship. The girl who graduates with this truth knows the reality of it.

God did, in fact, lead me into this ministry. This was not the plan that I had for my life. But in retrospect, if I had it to do over, this is what I would choose.

I remember that first meeting with 12 girls so clearly. I had prepared a lesson from the Old Testament Book of Ruth and had memorized it verbatim. The girls were moving around, brushing each other's hair, and whispering. I did not know what I was doing, but not one girl cared. They were excited to be there. I grew as a teacher as I continued to teach. God took me right where I was. The best thing I had going for me was the very definite fact that I loved each girl and wanted to be with her.

My dearest dear Donna,
Betty Jane and I cannot begin to express the thanks we have in our hearts for you. As you probably know by this time, the only things that are really meaningful in life are the things you

*do for other people. So when you give of yourself to my
daughter, gifts that I cannot pay you for, you burden my heart
with joy. As we look back on life, we can all remember teachers, friends, and special people who have shaped and molded
our lives. I'm sure as Emily reflects someday you will hold a
special place in her heart.*

*With all the love we can possibly muster in our hearts,
Betty Jane and I thank you for what you have done and for
what you will do with our child.*

*We love you in the name of Jesus,
H. Milner Snuggs, DMD*

Emily, whose father wrote that letter many years ago, is
now an adult with a daughter of her own who is ready for
Community Ministry for Girls. She has practiced leadership in so many ways, including serving as director for a
huge Vacation Bible School each summer. One seed
planted in Emily's life has been reproduced in the lives of
thousands of boys and girls. What a worthwhile investment.

Will you become that mentor for some girls you know?

Portions of this chapter are based on an article which first appeared in the
Briarword, a publication of Briarwood Presbyterian Church in Birmingham,
Alabama.

*Statistics for 1940 and 1982 appeared in the Indianapolis Tech Challenge
Newsletter, January 1983. Statistics for 1996–97 are from "Violence and Discipline Problems in U.S. Public Schools: 1996–97"; available at
http://nces.ed.gov/pubs98/violence/98030006.html; and http://nces.ed.gov/
pubs98/violence/tab10.html; Internet; accessed August 16, 2002.

Love one another deeply and from the heart—
A command from God—a blessing—an art.
Vulnerability, nakedness—joy and pain
Awkwardness to openness—no loss—great gain.
Walls so impenetrable box us in—
Separate, isolate, and closet our sin.
What a waste, a vapor, a façade—
Never the plan of our infinite God.

While sitting in church Resurrection Day,
God the strings of my heart did play.
At first, O so tight—they would not budge
Yet gently, consistently the Spirit did tug.
All preconceived ideas began to dissipate,
The armor was loosened and I could relate.
The condition of my heart was not the best—
God's MRI—His strongest test,
Revealed a heart pent up—not at rest.

The choice was mine—give in or resist,
Open my arms or close my fist.
Let my heart break and eyes swiftly flow—
Or "get a grip"—no emotion show.

"Confess your sins to one another that you might be
        healed"—
Not at all an absolute by which we are thrilled.
This involves the deepest part of all we are—
The layers, the covering, masks and scars.
This building has come over years—not just days,
Deception, self-deceit, and rationalizations play,
The screen of our lives—so paramount seen,
As the Master's light so piercingly beams.

My decision is made—I will let go.
A consent of my will but actions will show.
The choice was made on Easter Day
But choices will come in many ways.
Will I be honest, transparent—give my heart away?
Or lock the door, shut the windows and "in self" stay.

Thank you, dear Mallie, for being a part,
Of the practical lab for my heart.
For listening, questioning, and tuning in
To every thought and emotion that I did send.
Talking to you was truly a start
As you are familiar with so much of my heart.
In fact, I believe you're the acid test
If I seek to fool you, I've failed all the test.
If all is not well and I refuse to let you know—
If I love and appreciate you but don't let it show—
If I keep our conversation light and don't go deep,
All that God has shown me will end in defeat.

1

Creating the Ties That Bind

1

Creating the Ties That Bind

In June of 1998 I heard the words, "You have breast cancer," words that would forever change my life. After several mammograms, sonograms, and needle biopsies, my surgeon called to say, "Donna, it doesn't look good. Come see me in the morning and bring Mallie with you."

Mallie Lynn had been my close friend for many years. She knew me well, and my doctor was aware of this. Literally, hundreds of friends would play a part in my healing and recovery, but Mallie's role was unique. From the moment I was diagnosed, she took charge. Mallie acted with authority at a time when I was unable to move. She literally put the courage into me from that first diagnosis and continued to do so through chemotherapy and all of my surgeries.

When Mallie and I began to speculate about the many months of chemotherapy and surgeries I would face, through tears I asked, "Do you think everyone will burn out?"

"Do you mean me specifically?" she asked in return. "No, I'm in it for the long haul."

Creating ties that bind begins with *wanting* to be close. There is a cost—commitment. "A man of many companions may come to ruin, but there is a friend who sticks closer than a brother," the writer of Proverbs said (Prov. 18:24). It is that kind of commitment to friendship we hope to instill in girls God gives us the opportunity to mentor.

"After David had finished talking with Saul, Jonathan became one in spirit with David, and he loved him as himself" (1 Sam. 18:1).

Friendship is one of the greatest gifts God gives us. Few people choose to go through life alone. Most of us genuinely want to have close friends. But true friendships are hard work and take effort on both sides. Friendship involves daring to risk rejection and hurt. The deeper the friendship, the deeper the hurt can be; but the deeper the friendship, the deeper the joy we can experience.

"'My commandment is this: Love each other as I have loved you. Greater love has no one than this, that he lay down his life for his friends'" (John 15:12–13).

God created us to live in community and mirror the love of Christ in the ways we interact with each other. We're all on a journey through life and each of us has her own specific path to take. Some are on the mountain peaks while others trudge through the valleys. And then the tables are turned as circumstances change. A true friend is an encourager.

"Two are better than one, because they have a good return for their work: If one falls down, his friend can help him up. But pity the man who falls and has no one to help him up! Also, if two lie down together, they will keep warm. But how can one keep warm alone?" (Eccl. 4:9–11).

"A friend loves at all times, and a brother is born for adversity" (Prov. 17:17).

To encourage means "to inspire with courage." A true friend sees a need and seeks ways to encourage, and doesn't wait to be asked.

God gave us friendships to help us along life's journey. Many times it's easy to help someone with a task or project. But helping with emotional hurts and traumas can be much more difficult.

"Better is open rebuke than hidden love. Wounds from a friend can be trusted, but an enemy multiplies kisses" (Prov. 27:5–6).

For several years I taught Bible to junior high students in a Christian school. Very few days would pass each week without a crisis. Feelings were hurt on a daily basis. Conflict was the name of the game. Lunchtime would often become a counseling session or a heated debate. Many afternoons I sat and listened as each girl told her side of the story. The deeper the friendship, the longer the confrontation often became. If we could ever find the root of the problem, many times the wrongs could be righted. Wounds could unleash deeper love or forever ruin a relationship.

As we work through problems with friends, they help us to see our potential and we help them to see theirs. The more whole and complete we are personally, the better friend we can be. As mentors we must not only learn to be true friends to these girls but also to show them how to be true friends to one another.

Shannon and Bea were two high school students equally talented and beautiful. They were best friends.

Many times I attended pageants, recitals, and competitions involving both girls. Often Shannon was named first runner-up while Bea was named winner. Or, at the next pageant, Shannon wore the crown while Bea stood behind her. Often I would go backstage to offer congratulations at the conclusion of an event. The response was always the same. "Shannon, you were wonderful. I'm so proud of you."

"But did you see Bea? She was awesome!" Shannon would reply.

"Bea, you played the piano beautifully."

"But did you see Shannon's dance? She created it herself!" These girls constantly encouraged one another and pointed out the best in each other.

> *"Don't let anyone look down on you because you are young, but set an example for the believers in speech, in life, in love, in faith and in purity" (1 Tim. 4:12).*

When we are secure and happy within ourselves, we can better reach out to others. Bea and Shannon had a rare friendship. I'm certain there were times when one was truly sad about not being the winner, but it didn't show. Their love for each other was such a strong force.

Adolescent girls experience bonding and intimacy when they spend time with each other in atmospheres that are safe and conducive to vulnerability and openness as well as encourage them to build each other up rather than destroy each other.

> *"Do not be misled. Bad company corrupts good character"* (1 Cor. 15:33).

My phone rang at 3:30 A.M. The call was from an eighth-grade girl. "Donna," she said, "I'm somewhere I shouldn't be and I'm about to do something you wouldn't like. Come get me soon." With parents out of town, the party was going strong. This young girl knew she wouldn't be able to withstand the temptation and found a plan of escape. She became my child until her parents returned.

Adolescent peer pressure is so strong. It can be used for great good or great harm. It is easy to find out what a person is like by observing those with whom she spends her time. When we are not able to resist temptation, God provides us a way out.

"A man who has friends must himself be friendly" (Prov. 18:24 NKJV).

Robin cross-stitched a piece for me which hangs on my bathroom wall: "To have a friend you must 'bee' one." A vividly stitched bumblebee completes the picture. And that is so true. In order to have intimate, special friends, we must be the kind of friend we want to have.

What kind of friend should we be? Understanding. Compassionate. Able to feel what the other person is going through. A true friend is easy to talk to and accepts the person just as she is.

"Be devoted to one another in brotherly love. Honor one another above yourselves. . . . Rejoice with those who rejoice; mourn with those who mourn" (Rom. 12:10,15).

When I faced chemotherapy, I knew I would have to endure eight rounds, with each one becoming progressively more difficult. The girls in the high school Bible study groups were such friends to me. After each treatment, when I would feel weak, they would come to meetings with their pajamas on—bedroom slippers included. We would then celebrate the following week as another round of chemotherapy was coming but the ultimate goal of completion was nearer. Laura Katherine volunteered to shave her head if I lost all my hair. Now that goes *beyond* sharing sorrow.

In the early years of my ministry a woman called to ask if she could speak with me. "Can you keep a secret?" she asked immediately. And before allowing me to answer, she added with emphasis, "For life!" That's quite an order, but has been a lifetime goal—to be a person who can keep secrets. Lives have been shattered and reputations ruined through words that were spoken out of order. God wants us to be friends who are trustworthy. Trust takes a lifetime to build and can be so quickly lost.

"See to it that no one misses the grace of God and that no bitter root grows up to cause trouble and defile many" *(Heb. 12:15).*

A true friend will not hold a grudge—anger that is played over and over again in the mind. Anger turned inward becomes bitterness. The Bible warns us so clearly about its devastating effects. Bitterness hurts everyone, but most especially the one who is bitter. A grudge becomes very heavy, costly luggage.

"A sound heart is life to the body, but envy is rottenness to the bones" *(Prov. 14:30 NKJV).*

Intimacy builds through understanding, trust, and forgiveness. It doesn't come quickly, and on the deepest level is so rare. Friendships occur on many levels, and all can be good. But it's impossible to have hundreds of intimate friends. Even Jesus had friends who were closer to Him than others.

I like to remind the girls in the Bible study groups that at one time they didn't even know their closest friends. That is always a startling thought because we generally feel we have known each other forever. That's why it's so important to look around, take notice of the people around us, and watch out for those we do not know. If we don't, we might miss out on a wonderful, intimate friendship.

I used to attend a morning Bible study also attended by 300 other women. Each week I would speak to everyone I came in contact with, probably 70 people. One day I decided not to speak first. The result astounded me. Less than 10 women said hello to me. Why?

Friendship involves taking the initiative to start conversations without worrying about what people will think. By really paying attention, asking good questions, and learning and using people's names, we can begin meaningful relationships.

Many years ago when I became a flight attendant, we were trained to use names. In fact, we recorded the names of each passenger on a chart and learned to refer to it before addressing each person. What wonderful training! We were taught to use a person's name three times after being introduced so as not to forget it. But, if we did forget, we learned just to ask again. This early training translates so naturally as we establish personal relationships.

We start as acquaintances and then begin developing closer friendships. When we pray for the person, become honest about ourselves and our needs, and ask about the other person's needs and desires, we build bonds of friendship. And in Christian friendships we are able to be interdependent rather than dependent or codependent.

Rarely do we develop that deeply intimate relationship with a friend. We can't make it happen. It's a gift God gives us to make us more effective in His kingdom. Only being filled with the Holy Spirit and controlled by God can we love our friends as God wants us to. The closer we are to God, the more we will be able to love others. Vulnerable love and commitment come from having a stable intimate relationship with Christ, and this takes time, commitment, and a willingness to submit to His power. That's why relationships are so important.

2

What Makes Girls Tick, and What Ticks Them Off

2

What Makes Girls Tick, and What Ticks Them Off

I do not have a degree in counseling, but after almost 30 years of working with adolescent girls, I could easily qualify for an honorary certificate. I am not a mother, at least not in the biological sense. But people often refer to me as the "mother of the multitudes." Over the years I've recorded extensive notes on various subjects concerning adolescent girls. I've found that although the culture around us may change, the root problems adolescent girls face remain relatively similar from one generation to the next.

Various mothers' and parents' groups frequently ask me to speak since I have stood in the gap for so many girls as they have fought and struggled through adolescence. Often the subject is What Teenagers Wish Their Parents Knew. Mentors stand in the place of parents in some instances; but in most cases these faithful, loving friends stand with the parents, reinforcing what they have already taught at home. Many times parents have said, "Thank you for talking with my daughter. She won't listen to me." I don't pretend to have all the answers, but I do have a good idea about what makes girls tick, and what ticks them off!

Trust and confidentiality

Many times a teenager begins a conversation with, "Promise not to tell?" Adults who make this promise should keep it. When they do not, a girl tends to become secretive. Nothing can pry the truth from her. Girls don't like to be talked about, especially by adults. A girl feels so deeply betrayed if she hears that other adults have discussed her activities, character, or thoughts.

Nancy called me crying hysterically. She had come home and turned on her family's answering machine. Somehow actual phone calls had been recorded, and Nancy heard a ten-minute conversation between her mother and a friend in which they discussed Nancy at length. Her mother revealed conversations Nancy had told her in confidence. Walls shot up and tremendous damage was done. The wise writer of Proverbs said, "Whoever repeats the matter separates close friends" (Prov. 17:9).

It takes a teenager an average of 2 years to deeply trust an adult. Most youth leaders or mentors get discouraged and give up after only 18 months. They never receive the benefits of deeply established love and trust. Those who do should honor and guard this trust as the precious gift it is. What if a girl confides something that her mother deeply needs to know?

"Do you promise not to tell?" Lynn pleaded, as she began talking to me. In the course of our conversation she revealed that she was pregnant.

"Lynn, your mother really needs to know."

"No, you promised," she stubbornly replied. We talked a little more.

"Lynn, do you want me to go with you to tell your mom?" I asked her.

"No!"

We continued to talk, until finally my next question:

"Lynn, do you want me to tell your mother for you?"

That was the solution. I knew that I would play a big part in her life as she dealt with all she would face. Had I gone behind her back and simply revealed the information she had entrusted to me, she would have lost confidence in me at a time when she needed me most.

Identity and independence

Adolescents want independence. This is a growing time, a time of separation and self-identity. They like to express themselves with what they wear, how they talk, and how they act. They like to choose their own friends and activities. Peer influence is tremendous. A strong mentor can help them keep balance and perspective.

Adolescent girls march to the beat of a different drum. They have a reference to time that is all their own. Arguments can erupt when an adult wants a task completed on her timetable. I've learned that it's better to say, "Girls, by this evening I want you to have done . . . ," rather than, "Girls, get this done immediately!"

With freedom comes responsibility, and responsibility must be given and accepted. For example, in Community Ministry for Girls Bible study groups, the girls hold offices. One of the most important is being responsible for refreshments at meetings. This girl has sole responsibility for making sure that there are plenty of drinks and snacks each week. If she neglects her job of calling to remind those who volunteer to bring something, the entire group may go without snacks. I won't bail her out. And, believe me, the other girls will remind her after a week or two of nothing but water to drink.

I allow the girls to fail. I don't do their jobs for them. After showing them what to do and how to do it, I let it go while still supervising.

Communication

How important it is to keep the lines of communication open—to listen to what a girl is really saying! It speaks volumes to a girl when she knows you put her high on your priority list. But why is it that some of the best conversations happen in the middle of the night?

It was another beach trip. The time, 3:00 A.M. Jenny sat on the edge of my bed. "Donna, are you awake?" No answer.

"Donna, please be awake." I rolled over, trying to pull out of a deep sleep. I had never had a really deep conversation with this eighth-grade girl. Now she had chosen 3:00 A.M. for it to happen. Pouring her heart out to me, she ended by asking Christ to come into her heart. Several weeks later, she wrote me a letter: "Bible study has helped me in *every* way! But you have done so much too. I've met new people and learned more about God and Jesus, but in a fun and interesting way. I love to go and help the people at the nursing home or the children at your school."

I'm so glad I woke up that night.

Responding, not reacting

It's often so easy to react rather than respond, especially to the statements and actions of adolescents. Our reactions show us who we really are, what we're made of deep down.

Meredith, an eighth-grader in one of our Bible study groups, constantly cried out for attention and made group times difficult. She regularly acted out her anger. It was hard to act with love towards her. It took a lot of self-control to keep from reacting. Often I didn't "feel" love toward her but would act in a loving way.

After a most traumatic Bible study once, she wrote me the following letter: "Right now I am losing all my friends that I had from last year and some of the ones I got to be friends with at the starting of the year. There are a few reasons for me losing most of my friends, but they are mostly my fault. The main reason is my attitude. I need to change it bad. As long as I can remember, I've always kept my feelings inside. I had all this hate and love for people—but I kept it all inside so nobody could see it. It was like I was one person on the outside and another person on the inside. No one really ever knew the *real* me because I always covered it up. Also I felt like everything was my fault, and usually when I did something I blamed someone else. I felt lots of guilt, anger, and jealousy. Well, last May I found out my sister did drugs and alcohol since eighth grade. She went into a rehabilitation center and got help. In July I went there for a week. It was called family week. You learned how to talk about things to people. Every day we would have two therapy sessions, and every time we would start out with, 'How do you feel today?' The first day we were there it took two hours just to get through that question. I learned how to tell people how I feel. The first day I told them how I felt and I was the first one to start crying. Well, now I've started going back to my old attitude (the one before I went to family week). I can't get out of it."

Had I reacted to this girl in a negative way, she would never have shared her heart with me.

Compromise

Though it's easier said than done, I've learned not to major on the minors or nag. I like order and neatness. Most teenagers could care less. Trips could have been disastrous had I not learned to compromise.

I always have a place to keep all my things in order, and the girls know not to touch them. In turn I usually wade through mounds of clothes thrown to and fro across the room and let them live as they please. Many wonderful bonding experiences might never have occurred had I constantly been on them.

I've learned not to always demand my own way. Teenagers have great minds and come up with wonderful ideas. I hope I will always stay open to them and their ideas.

Consistency

Community Ministry for Girls is now in its second generation. I've watched the girls go through many growing pains and pull through. I've given them freedom with rules because true freedom comes in having boundaries. While cultural standards constantly change, and moral values no longer seem absolute, God's word is the same; and God is the same yesterday, today, and forever.

The key to any girl's heart is love and consistency. Christ is the only constant. Parents and mentors play a tremendous role in bridging the gap between adolescence and adulthood, but Christ is the North Star. A Christian mentor in an adolescent girl's life can be like a compass that points her to that Star.

3

Mentor, Leader, Friend

3

Mentor, Leader, Friend

"Do your best to present yourself to God as one approved, a workman who does not need to be ashamed and who correctly handles the word of truth" (2 Tim. 2:15).

Many years ago I took a group of girls to the beach. They had just finished the ninth grade. I met them in the school parking lot as school dismissed on the last day. Spirits were high as student after student hurried from the junior high into the bliss and freedom of summer.

Many well-meaning parents had warned me that this group of girls would give me trouble. A meeting with the girls and their mothers had preceded the trip. We set three rules—three absolutes: No smoking. No drinking. No going in other cars or condos without my permission. I was the adult responsible for the safety and morality of these 10, 14-year-old girls. All agreed to abide by the rules.

After we had been at the beach for less than a day, they begged me to take them to another beach. Apparently the really cute boys were there. It was evening. I finally agreed to go with the stipulation that we would return to our condo at my discretion. Pulling the van under the light of the parking lot, I opened my book to begin reading. That never happened. It didn't take long for me to realize that this was not a safe place for the girls to be.

Locking the van door, I began walking under the cloak of semidarkness as beer bottles broke around me and profanity rang clearly through the night air. Dressed like a teenager, I looked no different than the crowd. I passed easily among the different groups, looking and listening for my girls.

Hearing a familiar voice, I turned to see two of the young ladies under my charge, the glow of orange between two fingers of each right hand. I wanted to bolt, but I couldn't. I loved them too much to let this slide. Reaching from behind, I tightened my fingers around the wrists of each hand holding the cigarettes. Gasps came as mouths dropped opened. One girl quickly spoke. "Donna, do you want me to get the others?"

I could barely say yes before the tears began to flow—not just a trickle, but a flood. My heart felt like it was breaking. The girls I loved dearly and who loved me had betrayed me. I knew they had a reputation for being a little on the wild side but I never believed for a moment that they would disobey my rules, the rules we had all agreed on.

As one girl left to find everyone else, the other came running toward me. "Donna, my mother lets me smoke."

"I'm not your mother. You agreed to this," I replied as I walked to the van.

Needless to say, the ride across the bridge back to our condo that night was extremely long. I could barely see to drive amidst the deluge of tears. No one spoke a word.

Arriving at the condo, I asked the girls to sit in the living room. We sat. No one said a word. Finally my questions began. "Girls, how long have we been on this trip?" It had been less than 12 hours. "What were the rules you all

agreed to?" They answered. "How many have you broken?"
Heads hung low. I then began my circle around the room.

"Ellen, were you smoking?"

"Yes, ma'am."

"Were you drinking?"

"Yes, ma'am."

"Courtney, were you smoking?"

"Yes, ma'am."

"Were you drinking?"

"Yes, ma'am."

It was now Eleanor's time. "Were you smoking?"

"No, ma'am."

"Were you drinking?"

"No, ma'am."

Once more I heard gasps as mouths dropped open. Suzanne was next. When I asked the questions, she answered both precisely with, "No." The group supported her reply. "She really wasn't, Donna."

The dilemma had not ended. What would I do? Our agreement was that if a rule was broken, we would pack up the van and return to Birmingham. We had reservations for a week and had been at the beach less than a day. We had not even slept in a bed.

I turned the problem over to the girls themselves. "What would you do if you were in my place?" I asked them. My whole ministry was at stake. Nothing like this had ever happened on one of our trips. Next I gave each girl a piece of paper and a pen and asked each to separate from the others. I gave them one hour to write what they would do if they found themselves in my predicament. I asked that they not sign their names.

"I understand the way you feel and I am so upset about this too," wrote one girl. "I just hope you will understand how much pressure there is and understand why people fall for it. I know you'll do what you think is best and I know that is what is right, but I just hope that you will let us stay and just talk to you and that everyone will open up and we can have a good rest of the trip. I don't know what to tell you to do, but I know you will do what is best; and I love you for whatever happens. I am really so sorry this happened and I just pray that you won't hold it against anyone. We love you."

"I would like to say that you have been a great influence in my life and always will be," wrote another. "I know that some of us have sinned against you and God tonight. If we packed up and went home, I would give my family so much disappointment. I don't think that I could ever face you or them again. Please give me a second chance to become straight and try not to sin against God. Before we left, my mother said that she would be so embarrassed if I broke a rule. It would shame her. My mother and I fight so much that whatever she says I want to do the exact opposite, just to make her mad at me. I have been praying to God to help me."

And from another girl: "I'm really and truly sorry about what happened here tonight. And I just want to tell you that I love you so much and that you are really an important part of my life because I've learned so much from you and that it has worked. That's why I still haven't given into peer pressure. But if you weren't around, I don't know what I would have turned out to be. But about the people who smoked and drank, I really think the best thing that would really help is to take each of them individually and talk to them. I love you."

"I am sorry," wrote another girl. "I think we all know how much we have hurt you and I know you know who this is from. I guess we should sleep on it or maybe give us a second chance or have an earlier curfew for the people you saw. I love you. I know what I did was wrong because it was disobeying you. I'm sorry if it has made you lose your faith in us."

Another girl wrote: "Donna, you have done *so* much for all of us and there's no telling where we'd be without you. Every year the drinking and smoking and everything else get worse and worse. It's terrible! But there's not much we can do to stop it. We really need to pray about it and try to put a stop to all of it. Donna, the best thing you can do is to talk to us and preach to us because you know more about peer pressure and the Bible than any of us. I'm really trying to get away from all the peer pressure but I guess all we can do is try to ignore it and get away from it. Please continue to teach us better morals and never stop telling us to get away from all the drinking and smoking that goes on. Your taking us on this Florida trip means so much to me. Please, just keep teaching us. Donna, although we may not show it, you mean more to me and all of us than anyone in this world. I'm so glad that God has put you in the position you are in because without you we would be wilder. You are so special and I'm truly sorry for the way that we hurt you tonight."

That was an extremely hard night in the life of my ministry. I had never had girls blatantly disobey me when I was in charge. But this was also a turning point. We did not go home. I gave them another chance, knowing that I would be severely criticized regardless of the decision I made. I had to make the call by myself and stand alone. I loved the girls deeply, but I was not their peer. I was their friend, but I had to lead when they disobeyed. I cared more about their character than I did about my popularity with them. I was their mentor.

After reading the letters and praying, I made the decision that we would stay. Yells, hugs, and screams filled the room as the girls jumped up and down shouting triumphant thank-yous. Then all fell silent when I said, "Girls, when we arrive home I will give you 24 hours to tell your parents everything that happened. I will follow up with a phone call to each one." Faces fell but each one understood. That night 10, 14-year-old girls slept in the room with me. I couldn't get them to leave my side.

Girls want to feel secure—to know someone loves them. They want boundaries, rules, and absolutes; but they will tolerate none of this without relationships. Teenagers recognize who loves them.

Leaders of girls in their adolescent years must have vision, wisdom, decisiveness, courage, humility, patience, and a sense of humor. But the key ingredient is love, lots of love, and more love. A mentor's friendship is so important, but that adult must always set proper boundaries. Love does cover a multitude of sins. And the mentor/leader must continue growing as the girls do. A person cannot lead where she has not been. God is constantly looking for people who are faithful.

"This is how we know what love is: Jesus Christ laid down his life for us. And we ought to lay down our lives for our brothers" (1 John 3:16).

In order for adolescent girls to grow into healthy adults, they need love from family and friends. In our very fragmented, chaotic world, many are left to their own devices. Many young girls have no one to really talk to. They come home from school to an empty house. Television, stereos, computers, VCRs, and DVDs fill the void. In the past, many young girls would enjoy lemonade and cookies on the front porch with kindhearted grandmothers, aunts, or neighbors and spend afternoons sharing experiences of the school day. Conversations of support and encouragement were readily available. Listeners were available when the girls were ready to talk. That scenario is rare today.

Teenagers need people who are available to them on their own timetable. Some families offer communication, affection, structure, and protection. But many do not. Often that only happens when someone outside the family—a caring adult mentor—shows love and support. Even the best, most dedicated parents can benefit from other people becoming involved in their daughters' lives. And the influence of positive peer relations in a group of girls cannot be overemphasized. A parent's influence during adolescence is limited. Not all girls will allow their parents to make a difference in their lives at this time. Friends will have the greatest impact. One of the best things that can happen to a girl is to be surrounded by well-adjusted friends. How wonderful and beneficial for a teenage girl to have a mentor who is also her friend. A relationship of this kind is a true, long-term investment into the harvest of a young girl's life. It's even more special when the mentor is a friend to the girl's other friends. Together they form a sound support group providing safety in numbers and strength to go against the tide of negative peer pressure— the fear of the sneer of the peer.

A woman who can effectively mentor adolescent girls must be self-disciplined. This quality does not come at one time, but is instead one step at a time, as all areas of life come under discipline. Just as she will influence girls to do, she should also set goals and work with progress toward each goal. Discipline begins with doing first things first, and often that means doing that which is the most disagreeable. Structure and discipline pay off in all areas of life—mentally, physically, spiritually, and socially. A good leader leads by example. Nothing is more devastating for a teenage girl than seeing her "hero" fall. No one is perfect. Everyone will sin and make numerous mistakes, but self-discipline is a primary key for the success of true leadership.

Leadership is costly. The more effective the leader is, the higher the price she will pay. And she will pay this price over a lifetime. Self-sacrifice is a big part of this.

"'When he has brought out all his own, he goes on ahead of them, and his sheep follow him because they know his voice'" (John 10:4).

A leader should always be ahead of her followers. She should have the ability to make decisions when no one else can or will. Moses stood alone on the mount. He was often misunderstood and criticized. Prophets like Jeremiah, Jonah, and Enoch were lonely. So was the Apostle Paul. A mentor of adolescent girls must welcome friendship but be prepared to stand alone. While this is difficult, it is often necessary.

A mentor for teenagers is often tired. Her hours are different from those of other adults because teenagers' hours are so different. Girls often like to talk in the middle of the night. The mentor/leader must be able to accept criticism, control her actions and reactions, accept rejection, and not take everything personally. She faces regular pressure and demands on her time and emotions. A true leader cares more for the welfare of others than herself. She has sympathy and concern for the problems of the girls but directs their confidence to the Lord.

"Follow my example, as I follow the example of Christ" (1 Cor. 11:1).

Can you or I really say that? No one is perfect. Every leader will sin and make numerous mistakes along the way. Leadership comes not only with a high cost but also with a tremendous responsibility. "Jesus said to His disciples, 'Things that cause people to sin are bound to come, but woe to that person through whom they come. It would be better for him to be thrown into the sea with a millstone tied around his neck than to cause one of these little ones to sin. So watch yourselves'" (Luke 17:1–2).

In order to lead in a way that influences others spiritually and for eternity, a mentor of girls must be filled with the power of the Holy Spirit. It is God's Spirit who empowers, who gives wisdom and guidance for all events and situations that come along. Leadership is a gift. God may give it for leading hundreds or thousands, or for the investment in five lives or even one. It does not matter. If God calls a person to mentor and lead, He will equip the person with what she needs.

"Being confident of this, that he who began a good work in you will carry it on to completion" (Phil. 1:6).

4

The Word, the Mentor, and Relationships

4

The Word, the Mentor, and Relationships

"Then Jesus came to them and said, 'All authority in heaven and on earth has been given to me. Therefore go and make disciples of all nations, baptizing them in the name of the Father and of the Son and of the Holy Spirit, and teaching them to obey everything I have commanded you. And surely I am with you always, to the very end of the age'" (Matt. 28:18–20).

When I became a Christian as a 9-year-old child, this was the first verse that actually came alive in my heart. I knew that besides leading a person to the Lord, I should make that person a disciple. And to me that meant teaching that person what I knew. That was my 9-year-old philosophy of discipleship. So I taught my friends Bible verses, stories, and songs. I invited them to Sunday School and church. As the years have passed, I've learned so much more about discipleship and the commitment that it involves.

"I have been crucified with Christ and I no longer live, but Christ lives in me. The life I live in the body, I live by

faith in the Son of God, who loved me and gave himself for me" (Gal. 2:10).

Commitment to Christ comes at a great cost. It means dying to our own wills and being willing to do whatever God asks us to do. A committed person lives her life in Christ, through Christ, and because of Christ. This is an act of the will through surrender and obedience to Jesus Christ.

"Then Jesus said to his disciples, 'If anyone would come after me, he must deny himself and take up his cross and follow me'" (Matt. 16:24).

> Lord, I give up all my own plans and purposes,
> All my own desires and hopes,
> And accept Thy will
> For my life.
> I give myself, my life, my all
> Utterly to thee to be thine forever.
> Fill me and seal me
> With thy spirit.
> Use me as thou wilt, send me where thou wilt.
> Work out Thy whole will in my life
> At any cost
> Now and forever.

Elisabeth Elliot copied this prayer, written by missionary Betty Stam, in her Bible as a teenager. To me it accurately describes what discipleship involves.

The groups in Community Ministry for Girls are at their core discipleship groups. Commitment is critical for these or any discipleship groups to be strong and grow. Just as we pay a price for personal discipleship, there is also a price to pay for leadership of and involvement in a discipleship group. Jesus desires 100 percent commitment.

"For the eyes of the Lord range throughout the earth to strengthen those whose hearts are fully committed to him" *(2 Chron. 16:9).*

God can do more with 1 person who is 100 percent committed than with 100 who are 99 percent committed. Part of discipleship involves developing a disciplined devotional life. In order to really get to know God and His will for our lives, we must spend time with Him every day. Yet setting aside a quiet time with God on a consistent basis for prayer and Bible study is one of the hardest things for most Christians to do.

"Do not let this Book of the Law depart from your mouth; meditate on it day and night, so that you may be careful to do everything written in it. Then you will be prosperous and successful" (Josh. 1:8).

How a Christian develops and maintains her quiet time depends largely on personality. I started keeping a prayer journal when I was 13 years old. Every day I would write letters to God consisting of praise, thanksgiving, and prayers for others and myself. This became a habit for me that is still part of my life today. In fact, I can't imagine not taking the time to do this. It is my lifeline. "You know, I can miss writing in my prayer journal for one day; but if I skip two days, I'm just not myself," I once said to one of my good friends. But she replied, "No, Donna, you are yourself." And that is true. It is the Holy Spirit who fills my heart with the fruit of His Spirit. Love, joy, peace, patience, gentleness, goodness, meekness, faith, and self-control are not a part of my natural disposition. They are a reflection of Christ and come only by His power and grace in me.

Although each person's quiet time will be unique, certain elements are important. You can help the girls you mentor understand that

• A quiet time should occur daily. Good quality time is more important than quantity of time.

• An effective quiet time includes prayer and Bible reading.

• Prayer can include four areas, easily remembered by the acronym ACTS:

Adoration, or praise. "Let everything that has breath praise the Lord" (Psalm 150:6).

Confession, or acknowledging sin and seeking forgiveness. "If we confess our sins, he is faithful and just and will forgive our sins and purify us from all unrighteousness" (1 John 1:9).

Thanksgiving, or honest gratitude. "Give thanks in all circumstances, for this is God's will for you in Christ Jesus" (1 Thess. 5:18).

Supplication, or prayers for others and self. "'Ask and it will be given to you; seek and you will find; knock and the door will be opened to you'" (Matt. 7:7).

• Prayer is a two-way communication and involves listening to God as well as speaking to Him. Sometimes writing down thoughts that come to mind is helpful because often this is how God speaks to us. Because prayer involves listening, it is important at times when we pray to simply be still and quiet before the Lord. "My son, if you accept my words and store up my commands within you, turning your ear to wisdom and applying your heart to understanding, and if you call out for insight and cry aloud for understanding, and if you look for it as for silver and search for it as hidden treasure, then you will understand the fear of the Lord and find the knowledge of God" (Prov. 2:1–5).

•Bible reading is a must. Only two things will last forever—the word of God and the souls of people. Everything else will perish. "'All men are like grass, and all their glory is like the flowers of the field; the grass withers and the flowers fall, but the word of our Lord stands forever'" (1 Peter 1:24–25). From the psalmist we read, "I have hidden your word in my heart that I might not sin against you" (Psalm 119:11). And from Paul's writings: "Do your best to present yourself to God as one approved, a workman who does not need to be ashamed and who correctly handles the word of truth" (2 Tim. 2:15).

God's Word teaches us about God, His history, and His will for our lives. Discipleship must include the Bible. It must center on the Bible and measure everything against the truth of the Scriptures. The Bible is the one authority. "All Scripture is God-breathed and is useful for teaching, rebuking, correcting and training in righteousness, so that the man of God may be thoroughly equipped for every good work" (2 Tim. 3:16).

Many ingredients go into making a good discipleship leader. But God takes us where we are. He looks for faithfulness. I did not know what I was doing that first day of Bible study, but God took me where I was and continues to make me what He wants me to be. As a leader is faithful, God will entrust more.

Perhaps the most important quality of all is that of being filled with the Holy Spirit. The Spirit will not force Himself upon us. We must turn over control of the various areas of our lives to Him. This is a process and must continue over a lifetime. The teacher must be yielded to the Holy Spirit in order to lead.

"Therefore I urge you, brothers, in view of God's mercy, to offer your bodies as living sacrifices, holy and pleasing to God—this is your spiritual act of worship. Do not conform any longer to the pattern of this world, but be transformed by the renewing of your mind. Then you will be able to test and approve what God's will is—his good, pleasing and perfect will" (Rom. 12:1–2).

We can only turn over to Christ as much as we know. As a person gives over to what the Spirit shows, He shows them more. God shows us areas of our lives that need changing. We are the ones who deliver up our lives.

No leader will ever be perfect. God does not expect perfection. He expects obedience. Each person must seek the filling of God's Spirit, walk yielded to that Spirit, and walk in reliance to that Spirit.

As a teacher obeys God and seeks His will in her life, she develops good, productive relationships with others. Fellowship with God spills over into fellowship with others.

I'd rather see a sermon than hear one any day,
I'd rather one should walk with me than merely tell the
  way.
The eye's a better pupil and more willing than the ear,
Fine counsel is confusing, but example's always clear;
And the best of all the preachers are the men who live
  their creeds,
For to see good put in action is what everybody needs.

I soon can learn to do it if you'll let me see it done;
I can watch your hands in action, but your tongue too fast
  may run.
And the lecture you deliver may be very wise and true,
But I'd rather get my lessons by observing what you do;

For I might misunderstand you and the high advice you give,
But there's no misunderstanding how you act and how you live.

         (Edgar A. Guest, "I'd Rather See a Sermon")[1]

Jesus said, "'If you hold to my teaching, you are really my disciples'" (John 8:31). And the early Old Testament teaching is still as important today as it ever was: "Impress them on your children. Talk about them when you sit at home and when you walk along the road, when you lie down and when you get up" (Deut. 6:7).

An effective discipleship group is Christ-centered and lifts high the word of God. Its leader knows Christ personally and lives up to the responsibility she is given with God's help. She builds relationships among the girls that go the distance, bonds that last a lifetime.

---

[1]Edgar A. Guest, "I'd Rather See a Sermon," *Collected Verse of Edgar A. Guest* (Chicago: Contemporary Books, Inc., 1934), 599.

5

The Bible and Today's Girls

5

The Bible and Today's Girls

I really want to thank you for helping me study the Bible. My mom and stepdad don't go to church or have a relationship with God. Even though they don't, my real dad is a good Christian. I'm trying to have God in my life. Bible study really helps. Before Bible study, I didn't have God in my heart at all. You've helped me realize that God is the key to a happy life! I pray every night that God will help my mom and stepdad to know God and have Him in their hearts. I know God is making me stronger and drawing me closer by doing this. Donna, it's like you've given me the key to God's house so now I can go inside, while for 12 years I've been sitting and waiting at the front door.

—from a 12-year-old

I am having a great time, but college is much more of an awakening than I thought it would be. One thing that really amazed me was a program they had during orientation. Basically, it was to promote safe sex on campus. They addressed issues such as, "You will be humiliated if you sleep together on a one-night stand. Wait about three weeks." I was in shock! To have authority figures encourage me and my peers to sleep around astounded me. I am so glad that I established and

kept my values through high school and now I see how it is
going to pay off.
      —from a college freshman

College . . . the word has been a part of my vocabulary for as
long as I can remember. I have always looked at it as part of
my future, as something that I would deal with later, not now.
I thought that I would be mature and able to handle all
aspects of life easily when my time came to go off to college.
Well, suddenly, before even realizing it, my time came. Is col-
lege different from high school? I think it depends on where
you go, whom you go with, and your relationship with Christ
when you arrive. I have finally realized that Christ is the only
way to get by not only schoolwise, but in all aspects of life here
in college and elsewhere. I really encourage all people to really
work on making their relationships right with Christ and as
strong as possible. It is important to have your whole life
under Christ's control before college, so when it's hard making
the transition of a new school and a new place, you don't have
to worry about trying to fit God in because this way He just
fits in naturally, out of your own free will, just out of habit.
      —from a college freshman

The excerpts above, taken from actual letters from girls,
demonstrate the value of God's Word in a girl's life. In
order for a girl to begin to know who she is, she must
know whose she is. God's Word gives her that foundation
and direction. God's Word is constant. God's Word is consistent. God's Word answers the questions of life.

> *"All Scripture is God-breathed and is useful for teaching,*
> *rebuking, correcting and training in righteousness, so that*
> *the man of God may be thoroughly equipped for every*
> *good work" (2 Tim. 3:16).*

God's Word provides us with wise counsel. It is our guide, a road map of life.

"Your word is a lamp to my feet and a light for my path" *(Psalm 119:105).*

There are so many paths in life that a teenage girl can take. Many are disastrous and lead to loneliness, frustration, destructive addictions and habits, even death. But God's road leads to life.

"'The thief comes only to steal and kill and destroy. I have come that they may have life, and have it to the full'" *(John 10:10).*

Christ shows us how to get on the road, warns us when we get off the path, shows us how to get back on it, and leads us to stay on that journey that God has designed for our lives, a journey filled with adventures and fulfillment. God's Word gives practical guidance and instruction on how to lead a life of purpose, joy, peace, and meaning.

"'Heaven and earth will pass away, but my words will never pass away'" *(Mark 13:31).*

The Bible, God's eternal Word, will exist forever and ever. Nothing can destroy it. Although it is a guide to life, we cannot grasp its real meaning apart from the enlightenment of the Holy Spirit.

A college professor continued to belittle the Bible day after day in the history class he taught. A Christian student became more and more outraged as she listened to this professor sacrifice God's Word on the altar of higher education. Finally, unable to stand it anymore, she stood and boldly spoke. "Sir, the Bible is a love letter written to Christians. The reason you don't understand it is the fact that you are reading someone else's mail."

The Bible comes to life when the Holy Spirit indwells the heart of a believer.

"And this is the testimony: God has given us eternal life, and this life is in his Son. He who has the Son has life; he who does not have the Son of God does not have life" (1 John 5:11–12).

Our starting point is at the Cross. This is where life begins. I like to use the illustration of the light bulb. There it sits, tightly secured within the lamp. It is not broken and appears to be in perfect order. Yet there is no life, no light until the switch is activated, causing energy-giving electricity to flow. This makes all the difference between light and darkness.

God gives eternal life, and we can have that life because of the sacrificial death and resurrection of Jesus Christ. Everyone who has accepted this finds eternal life. Without the life of the Holy Spirit darkness and death exist.

A girl's journey of discovery into knowing who she is begins with knowing whose she is. And this begins with a personal commitment of faith in Jesus Christ.

"But these are written that you may believe that Jesus is the Christ, the Son of God, and that by believing you may have life in his name" (John 20:31).

God gave us His Word to lead us to belief in Christ, which in turn leads us to eternal life.

"But God demonstrates his own love for us in this: While we were still sinners, Christ died for us" (Rom. 5:8).

God loves us so much that in spite of our sin and rebellion, He sent Jesus to pay the penalty for that sin and rebellion on the Cross.

"'Greater love has no one than this, that he lay down his life for his friends'" (John 15:13).

Sin drove Jesus Christ to the Cross: the sin of the world and our own personal sin.

"But your iniquities have separated you from your God; your sins have hidden his face from you, so that he will not hear" (Isa. 59:2).

God came to us through the person of Jesus Christ. The Lord of the universe became flesh and lived among people. He who was without sin became sin for us so that we could live eternally with Him.

"For Christ died for sins once and for all, the righteous for the unrighteous, to bring you to God. He was put to death in the body but made alive by the Spirit" (1 Peter 3:18).

The death of Jesus Christ was effectual for everyone: one death for the lives of all for all time. Although no other sacrifice ever will be needed, eternal life is a gift and must be accepted.

"Yet to all who received him, to those who believed in his name, he gave the right to become children of God" (John 1:12).

Suppose I hold a beautiful package wrapped in brightly colored paper, tied with a crisp full bow. Many admire its beauty as I stand, hands held open, offering it to any taker. The package becomes a gift to the one who reaches out and receives it. It becomes her own. Jesus offers His gift of salvation to anyone who reaches out and accepts His gift of eternal life.

"I tell you the truth, whoever hears my word and believes him who sent me has eternal life and will not be condemned; he has crossed over from death to life" (John 5:24).

Three things happen as a result of hearing and believing. A person is forever changed—present, future, and past. She has eternal life. She will not be condemned and she has crossed over from death to life. The transaction happens immediately upon accepting Christ as Lord and Savior. Once a girl has crossed over, the light switch has been activated and she is able to begin to hear the voice of the Lord.

"My sheep listen to my voice; I know them, and they follow me. I give them eternal life, and they shall never perish; no one can snatch them out of my hand. My Father, who has given them to me, is greater than all; no one can snatch them out of my Father's hand" (John 10:27–29).

God gives us eternal life, which is a life of abundance as we now have the ability to hear God's Word as it relates to our lives.

"Therefore, if anyone is in Christ, he is a new creation; the old has gone, the new has come" (2 Cor. 5:17).

The Bible is an extension of God Himself.

> *"In the beginning was the Word, and the Word was with God, and the Word was God. . . . The Word became flesh and made his dwelling among us" (John 1:1,14).*

We were created for God—to live in His presence and enjoy Him forever. As a girl reads, studies, and meditates upon God's Word, her life is transformed. She begins to see herself from God's perspective and her questions are answered.

> *"Do not conform any longer to the pattern of this world, but be transformed by the renewing of your mind. Then you will be able to test and approve what God's will is— his good, pleasing and perfect will" (Rom. 12:2).*

"Who am I?" adolescent girls often ask. I am a child of God, a royal princess, an inheritor of the kingdom. I am made in the image of God for His glory. The Bible helps a girl to look deep within her soul in order to find and begin to know her true self. She learns to acknowledge her own unique gifts and accept her feelings and limitations. She begins to make decisions about values, standards, and commands from God. What is socially acceptable does not necessarily match with God's Word. The Bible teaches her a process, which includes knowing the difference between thinking and feeling, between hearing her own voice and that of another person rather than the will of the Lord. God's Word shows a girl the difference between immediate gratification and long-term goals. Culture may change but God's guidelines do not. They help a girl chart a course based upon that road which, although narrow, leads to joy, confidence, personal satisfaction, and peace.

Our world tells a girl to be true to her own North Star: Follow the ways of your heart and do what is best for you. So many voices—the media, peers, teachers, entertainers, athletes—contribute to the messages adolescents hear. Often these voices conflict and confuse, tossing them to and fro. They need something to cling to, to hold onto with all their might. In order to make it through life in a productive, satisfying, fulfilling way, a girl must stay on the path. To do this, she must know who she is, her standards and values. True freedom comes in knowing the truth and staying true to it.

"You will know the truth, and the truth will set you free" (John 8:32).

Truth begins when a girl accepts Christ as Lord and Savior. God's Word begins to come alive and girls are able to trust that source as the meaning and direction in their lives. This is the rock to which they can cling, their North Star. The Bible can and does meet the needs of girls where they are today and where they will be in the future.

"Faith comes from hearing the message, and the message is heard through the word of Christ" (Rom. 10:17).

How important to invest in the lives of girls while they are young! Seeds planted early in their lives help them grow into healthy, mature, stable young women.

6

Lessons in Love, Grace, and Beauty

.6.

Lessons in Love, Grace, and Beauty

"Charm is deceptive, and beauty is fleeting; but a woman who fears the Lord is to be praised" (Prov. 31:30).

Appearance, popularity, and status are so important in our culture, particularly among adolescents. How a person looks determines in many cases the degree to which others accept him or her. God's love and acceptance of us is so different from this standard. He loves and accepts us just as we are. Nothing can change that fact. God designed each of us and made us to His own exact specifications. He designed us in His image for His glory. We can never make Him love us any more or any less than He already does.

Though our culture sends adolescent girls very different messages about beauty, clothing, and style, the most important personal qualities are spiritual, not physical. Proverbs 31 paints a very beautiful picture of a godly woman, someone who works hard, has virtuous qualities, and provides for her family as well as the community. She is a wonderful mother and a faithful wife. Everyone admires her. The godly woman is clothed with strength and dignity. She is filled with wisdom, humility, righteousness, mercy, and a reverent fear of the Lord. Honor accompanies all of these attributes. Her home is beautiful and orderly as she makes God the first priority in her life.

The New Testament further describes the kind of beauty God desires in us: "Do not let your beauty be that outward adorning of arranging the hair, of wearing gold, or of putting on fine apparel; but let it be the hidden person of the heart, with the incorruptible ornament of a gentle and quiet spirit, which is very precious in the sight of God" (1 Peter 3:3–4 NKJV).

Lessons in Love and Grace

Real, lasting beauty begins within. Surface beauty is vain and has no real importance or lasting value. Beautiful clothes and good grooming can never compensate for lack of inner grace. The good news is that God offers us His eternal, spiritual clothing. "For we are God's workmanship, created in Christ Jesus for good works, which God prepared in advance for us to do" (Eph. 2:10). The prophet Isaiah said, "I delight greatly in the Lord; my soul rejoices in my God. For he has clothed me with garments of salvation and arrayed me in a robe of righteousness" (Isa. 61:10).

What we think about ourselves—our self-esteem—is determined by what we know about ourselves. Many adolescents (and some adults), unfortunately, listen not to the voice of God but to the voices of their peers and the media as they form opinions about themselves. A truly positive self-image comes from accepting the way God made us as well as accepting the circumstances in which He has placed us.

A negative self-image comes from comparisons with other people. When an adolescent girl compares herself with her friends, she will always feel either superior or inferior, and neither is realistic or Christlike. A negative self-image can result in an inability to trust God and can make other deep relationships difficult or even impossible. If a girl rejects herself, she expects others to do the same to her. She may begin to focus on things that really don't matter, just to fill in the broken places of her heart. In order to really love other people, a girl must learn to love and value herself as God does.

How does this happen? It happens when girls realize that God loves and accepts them just as they are. No matter what they have done, God will forgive them and literally wipe the record clean. "If we confess our sins, he is faithful and just to forgive us our sins and purify us from all unrighteousness" (1 John 1:9). And from the prophet Isaiah, "I, yes, I alone am he who blots away your sins for my own sake and will never think of them again" (Isa. 43:25).

Inner beauty begins with a brand-new heart. "'I will give you a new heart and put a new spirit in you; I will remove from you your heart of stone and give you a heart of flesh'" (Ezek. 36:26). It's just as if someone has turned on the lights. Everything looks different. Attitudes change. God's salvation and presence in our lives allow us to see things from God's point of view rather than our own. We want to please God, and He gives us strength to do this through the power of His Holy Spirit. When we sin, we ask for and receive forgiveness, and God restores our joy. The Bible starts to come alive for us, and God speaks to us through His Word.

Best of all God's love is now poured in our hearts. It begins with love for the Lord, then overflows to those around us. We become real people. We feel good about ourselves when we look good, do well, are accepted by others, and succeed. And we feel best about ourselves as we stay in the center of God's will. We look to Him and not ourselves as we know and obey His commands.

The inner grace God gives us through His love results in outward beauty. Regardless of how physically beautiful an adolescent girl is, she will never be winsome and charming without cultivating a beautiful spiritual posture. Though light in step herself, people will look at her in a totally different light if she walks all over them. She may have a regal appearance, but if she holds her head high in conceit and arrogance, others will not be attracted to her. Graceful body motions do not compensate for a girl who is rude, prideful, deceitful, disloyal, and dishonest. An adolescent girl who seeks to please God is honest, wise, and humble. She walks circumspectly, uprightly, by faith in truth and in the Spirit.

Perhaps a girl's greatest enemy as she learns lessons in grace is her tongue. The tongue is one of the most powerful members of our body. It has an amazing capacity for both good and evil. Consider these insights from the Scriptures: "We all stumble in many ways. If anyone is never at fault in what he says, he is a perfect man, able to keep his whole body in check. When we put bits into the mouths of horses to make them obey us, we can turn the whole animal. Or take ships as an example. Although they are so large and are driven by strong winds, they are steered by a very small rudder wherever the pilot wants to go. Likewise the tongue is a small part of the body, but it makes great boasts. Consider what a great forest is set on fire by a small spark" (James 3:2–5).

And the writer of Proverbs said, "The tongue has the power of life and death" (Prov. 18:21).

Our tongues have the power to kill or destroy. Words hurt feelings, destroy reputations, and break confidences. But because the tongue is such a powerful thing, it can work for good if used in the right way. It can encourage and build up others. The godly woman, according to Proverbs 31:26, "speaks with wisdom, and faithful instruction is on her tongue."

> *"The good man brings good things out of the good stored up in his heart. . . . For out of the overflow of his heart his mouth speaks" (Luke 6:45).*

Whatever is in our hearts determines what comes out of our mouths. If we really love others from the heart with God's love, then this will overflow through our words and actions. We become people of love, reflecting the love God has shown to us: "Love is patient, love is kind. It does not envy, it does not boast, it is not proud. It is not rude, it is not self-seeking, it is not easily angered, it keeps no record of wrongs. Love does not delight in evil but rejoices with the truth. It always protects, always trusts, always hopes, always perseveres. Love never fails" (1 Cor. 13:4–8).

The world has many different ideas about love. Some describe it in terms of feelings, but God's love is much more than a vague idea. It is an attitude that we express by our lives and actions. God's love in us enables us to be patient with others. "Therefore, as God's chosen people, holy and dearly loved, clothe yourselves with compassion, kindness, humility, gentleness and patience. Bear with each other and forgive whatever grievances you may have against one another" (Col. 3:12).

We can easily show kindness and forgiveness because we have experienced it from God. "Be kind and compassionate to one another, forgiving each other, just as in Christ God forgave you" (Eph. 4:32). We sincerely desire the happiness and welfare of others. This attitude comes from within and causes us to be sensitive to the needs of others. Kindness expresses what love can no longer hold in. It sees a need and seeks to meet it in another person's life.

God's love in us wants the best for the other person. We are not envious, resentful, or bitter. "For where you have envy and selfish ambition, there you will find disorder and every evil practice" (James 3:16).

Because of God's love in us, we do not seek personal gain or try to impress others. Instead, we seek to give glory to Jesus Christ. "May I never boast except in the cross of our Lord Jesus Christ, through which the world has been crucified to me, and I to the world" (Gal. 6:14).

We can have a proper attitude about ourselves and base our self-image on our relationship with Christ. "Your attitude should be the same as that of Christ Jesus: Who, being in the very nature God, did not consider equality with God something to be grasped, but made himself nothing, taking the very nature of a servant, being made in human likeness. And being found in appearance as a man, he humbled himself and became obedient to death—even death on a cross!" (Phil. 2:5–8).

God's love in us truly affects everything we say and do and causes us to treat others with courtesy and respect. "As a prisoner for the Lord, then, I urge you to live a life worthy of the calling you have received. Be completely humble and gentle; be patient, bearing with one another in love. Make every effort to keep the unity of the Spirit through the bond of peace" (Eph. 4:1–3).

When we love as Christ loves, we do not insist on having our own way. We understand that sometimes it's better to be loving than to be right. We desire the ultimate good of the other person ahead of having our own emotions satisfied. "'The Lord, the Lord, the compassionate and gracious God, slow to anger, abounding in love and faithfulness'" (Ex. 34:6).

The person who loves with Christlike love thinks the best of other people instead of holding a record of the times she was wronged. She rejoices when God's truth is lifted up. As an agent of God's love, she works to preserve and protect. Her love knows no end to trust. She always believes in the person she loves. Her love is able to withstand all obstacles, even the possibility of not having her love returned. She can love this confidently because her source of love is God, and God is love. Her love is eternal and permanent because God is eternal and permanent.

As a young girl begins to plant seeds of lasting value, her character will grow. As she directs her life toward love, she will be filled with love to keep giving away. "'A new commandment I give to you: Love one another. As I have loved you, so you must love one another. By this all men will know that you are my disciples, if you love one another'" (John 13:34–35).

"This is how we know what love is: Jesus Christ laid down his life for us. And we ought to lay down our lives for our brothers. If anyone has material possessions and sees his brother in need but has no pity on him, how can the love of God be in him? Dear children, let us not love with words or tongue but with actions and in truth" (1 John 3:16–18).

"Finally, brothers, whatever is true, whatever is noble, whatever is right, whatever is pure, whatever is lovely, whatever is admirable—if anything is excellent or praiseworthy—think about such things" (Phil. 4:8).

Lessons in Beauty, Inside and Out

God knows all our thoughts and all our ways and is

concerned about every detail. He is with us wherever we go and will never leave us or forsake us. God fashioned, knew, and loved us even before we were born. God Himself, the Lord of the universe, constantly thinks about us.

"O Lord, you have searched me
and you know me.
You know when I sit and when I rise;
You discern my going out and my lying down;
you are familiar with all my ways.
Before a word is on my tongue
you know it completely, O Lord.
You hem me in—behind and before;
you have laid your hand upon me.
Such knowledge is too wonderful for me,
too lofty for me to attain.
Where can I go from your Spirit?
Where can I flee from your presence?
If I go to the heavens, you are there;
if I make my bed in the depths, you are there.
If I rise on the wings of the dawn,
if I settle on the far side of the sea,
even there your hand will guide me,
your right hand will hold me fast.
If I say, 'Surely the darkness will hide me
and the light become night around me,'
even the darkness will not be dark to you;
the night will shine like the day,
for darkness is as light to you.
For you created my inmost being;
you knit me together in my mother's womb.
I praise you because I am fearfully and wonderfully made;
your works are wonderful,
I know that full well.

My frame was not hidden from you
when I was made in the secret place.
When I was woven together in the depths of the earth,
your eyes saw my unformed body.
All the days ordained for me
were written in your book
before one of them came to be.
How precious to me are your thoughts, O God!
How vast is the sum of them!
Were I to count them,
they would outnumber the grains of sand"
(Psalm 139:1–18).

While everything around us might tell us to listen to what other people say as we determine what we think about ourselves, the Bible tells us differently. In order for girls to listen to God's voice in this and other matters, they must have opportunities to hear and recognize His voice. The girl who knows who she is and whose she is has an inner beauty that flows to the outside. Her life becomes a light.

Our culture has no doubt gone overboard with fads, fashion, and appearance. While it's wrong to place too much emphasize on appearance and styles, it's also wrong not to be concerned at all. The key is balance. Adolescent girls need to learn what it means to be beautiful from the inside out, godly young women. Proverbs 31 makes reference to three areas that concern a godly woman physically:

Her health. "She sets about her work vigorously; her arms are strong for her tasks" (Prov. 31:17).

Her appearance. "She is clothed in fine linen and purple" (Prov. 31:22).

Her home. "She makes coverings for her bed" (Prov. 31:22).

Directly after graduation from the University of Alabama, I headed for Euless, Texas, to attend the stewardess training for a major American airline. (We were *stewardesses* then, not *flight attendants,* the term used today.)

Before arriving at the school I was expected to meet certain criteria and I understood that fully. Months before I left home, I received an instructional manual and had read and reread every word. I knew I must be thin. I knew my skin must be clear and my overall appearance neat. Aside from that, I need not worry for professional experts would work with every girl in the class for five and a half weeks. A series of interviews had preceded my acceptance so I knew that I was chosen by the airline to represent their company. "You are our hostesses. The passengers remember you." I heard that statement over and over. I knew that I would learn a lot about personal appearance but could never have imagined how much. Nothing was left undone.

Every day we attended classes where we learned how to walk, how to talk, how to sit, and how to stand. Specialists worked with our makeup, hairstyles and color, and fingernails. We were weighed every single day.

At first we had a lot of fun. But after a while, my entire class began to experience burnout. I remember telling my roommates that I felt I was becoming too self-centered and vain.

One morning our head instructor addressed our class. "Girls, we have put you through some very rigorous training. You've learned well your duties as a stewardess. Each of you should feel confident of being able to meet the needs of your passengers should medical problems or emergencies arise. You know how to serve and be a good hostess. I know you are all tired of working on your personal appearance. Each one of you has received advice and constructive criticism. You can now be certain that you look the best you could ever look. Now, get out there, forget yourself, and reach out to your passengers!"

I'll never forget that statement. It was true! I only felt self-conscience when I didn't look good—like the time my alarm didn't go off and I overslept for an early morning flight. I made it, barely, and truly looked like something the cat dragged in.

As Christians, our inward condition, outward appearance, and the condition of the area where we live all give testimony to God. Certain disciplines in each of these areas help us be our best. When I graduated from stewardess school, we were told, "The training and discipline you learned will go with you throughout your life." They were right! They trained me well and I've never lost that discipline.

In order to have and maintain good health, a girl needs a proper diet, adequate sleep, proper exercise, and good hygiene. Today most girls—and women—must exercise intentionally because they don't get enough physical activity in their daily routines. Our lifestyles are very different from that of the Proverbs 31 woman, who walked many miles a day looking for materials to make fabrics, providing for the needs of her household, taking care of vineyards, shopping for goods she needed, and delivering her goods to various merchants (not to mention all of the energy she expended by spinning and weaving!). A girl of today may rarely walk, instead riding in or driving a car. Aerobics classes and 10K runs were not necessary in Bible days.

An adolescent girl needs to understand that her body is the temple of the Holy Spirit and she is bought with a high price. Anything that might hurt her body is wrong for her: drugs, alcohol, cigarettes, premarital sex, overeating, undereating. Self-control is a fruit of the Spirit.

Just as we must exercise discipline about what we put into our bodies, we should also exercise discipline about what we put on them. Adolescent girls who are Christians are daughters of the King, and that fact should affect how they dress. Balance is so important. We don't want to go to either extreme of becoming overly concerned or not concerned enough about clothing. What is fashionable or faddish may not be appropriate and may not be the best investment for a good wardrobe.

In Community Ministry for Girls, we have helped girls understand and achieve balance when it comes to beauty and fashion through fashion shows. Local department stores and fashion consultants have been glad to help us with these presentations for the girls. One time we combined this with a beautiful luncheon where over 100 eighth- and ninth-grade girls, wearing their best dresses, participated. Round tables were decorated with pink and white linen cloths. Balloons of silver, lavender, and pink rose high in the center of each table.

After a nice lunch, the girls listened to a speaker talk about being beautiful inside and out. Following that, racks of the latest clothing were wheeled into the room. A fashion consultant showed the girls various styles and told them which looked best on which figures. She then taught them how to buy wisely, how to mix and match pieces, and how to choose appropriate colors according to skin tones and complexions. Many of the girls modeled the fashions as she spoke. Next, a cosmetics specialist spoke about skin care and gave samples of several products. Local merchants donated door prizes, which girls received at the end.

Like appearance and overall health, posture also sends a message about who we are, how we feel about ourselves, and, as Christians, reflects our relationship with Christ.

Poor posture can indicate laziness, discouragement, indifference, and lack of confidence, while a lovely posture, graceful carriage, and pleasant facial expressions can communicate confidence, good self-esteem, cheerfulness, and an ability and desire to be of service. As Christians, we have a responsibility to bring honor to Christ in all we do. "So whether you eat or drink or whatever you do, do it all for the glory of God" (1 Cor. 10:31).

A girl must feel good about herself and the way she looks in order to reach out effectively to others. Many of the most attractive girls are not necessarily the most beautiful. Actions make a person beautiful, not just appearance.

One of the service projects growing from the Bible studies of the ministry involves visitation to various nursing homes. On one occasion, we were planning a trip for Valentine's Day. It was the week after we had a lesson on outer beauty. As an experiment, I asked the girls to carefully look at the faces of the residents. "Look at the lines in their skin," I encouraged them. "Are they smile lines? Are they frown lines? So much of a person's character is seen in the lines of time that mark their faces."

Mrs. Pittman, over 100 years old, was a favorite of the girls. On this occasion, I went to her bed. She appeared to be sleeping but the nurses encouraged me to wake her. I had to yell her name several times before she opened her eyes. A caretaker carefully got her up, combed and braided her very long hair, put her in the wheelchair, and rolled her out into the hall. All the girls were waiting and started singing very loudly, "Jesus Loves Me." Mrs. Pittman sang along. We gave her candy, which she loved, but she insisted that she should eat only one piece. As she peeled back the wrapper of the chocolate, I pointed out her very slender fingers and remarked to the girls that she had once been a very accomplished pianist. I told them that she had loved and served Jesus all her life. Neatly placing the candy wrapper in her lap, she asked, "Want to sing?"

"What do you want to sing, Mrs. Pittman?" I yelled back.

"Amazing Grace," came her reply. We all sang the first verse and then Mrs. Pittman sang the last as loudly as she could:

> When we've been there ten thousand years,
> Bright shining as the sun,
> We've no less days to sing God's praise
> Than when we first begun.

When we finished singing, she pointed to the girls and said, "Jesus loves you." That thin, delicate finger then pointed to her heart as she said, "Jesus loves me." Her head then bowed. Mrs. Pittman never spoke another word while in this world. She went to be with Jesus, her Lord and Savior, the next day.

7

Lessons in Serving Others

7

Lessons in Serving Others

"Therefore, as we have opportunity, let us do good to all people, especially to those who belong to the family of believers" (Gal. 6:10).

When I was a child, Daddy would often tell me, "I don't care if you ever make a dime. Just give your life away." One of the greatest blessings of being healthy and alive is the ability to serve, to reach out to others, to see a need and meet it. We are all self-centered by nature; especially is this true of adolescents. Serving God by serving others helps us take our eyes off of ourselves. Once we realize that God wants to and can work through us to meet others' needs, there's no end to the difference we can make in the world.

When I was a Bible teacher in a Christian school, I read aloud to my class on Fridays. A favorite author was Ann Kiemel. The junior high students loved to listen to her stories of how God worked in everyday situations. One day I decided that we should all experiment with this very thing. I asked each student to think of a way that he or she could reach out and serve someone else. They were to write up their plans and turn them in to me on the following Monday. The next week I assigned another essay, this time describing the results. Did the plan work? Why or why not? It really didn't matter what the outcome was. The point of the project was that they serve. This continued for the next six weeks. The students became more and more excited and creative.

We then decided that every person would write Ann Kiemel a letter describing his or her favorite service project. We wrapped over 100 letters for mailing and sent them on their way to Ann. She wrote back (in her lowercase style):

dear donna and students,

i have just returned from a trip to the west coast, speaking, and received your packet of letters. it has been such a thrill. even though i had many other pieces of mail, i sat down and went through every single one of the letters each one of you wrote me. you are so creative and brilliant. you made me laugh and cry. you made me feel warm and wonderful. you made me know that God can move the world through you too. after reading all of your messages, i knew we were really a team and Jesus really is our hope and together we're going to do a lot in His name. donna, you must be a great teacher. thank you for so believing with me, for sharing my dreams so personally with your students. it has really been a thrill for me, and frankly i am overwhelmed. today it was just what i needed to be encouraged and to believe that all I am trying to do is making a difference. i wish i had a teacher like you when I had been in 7th or 8th grade. Your students show such individuality and wisdom, and they all seem to have real hearts for God. they will never be able to walk away from that whatever else may come into their lives. . . . the greatest thing in all the world really is loving and serving Jesus Christ.

> *joyfully,*
> *ann kiemel*

Months later the students were still sharing with me their ideas and projects. They had experienced the tremendous blessings that come when you give your life away.

The service God commands of us is not boring or tedious. In fact, it can be a lot of fun. As the students found out, the possibilities are endless.

Adult mentors and leaders are the keys to getting adolescents excited and motivated for service. By definition, a leader must lead. She can't take the group where she is unable to go herself. I generally choose service projects in areas that fit my personality and often mesh them with what is going on in my own life at the time.

For example, for years I ran and trained for marathons and 10K races. The girls in the ministry got excited about this and wanted to have their own runs, so we planned a two-mile fun run which brought in over $3,000 for the next 2 consecutive years, money we gave to a home for abused women and children. The newspaper ran an 8-by-10 picture of the girls, ribbons streaming and flying in the breeze, with the caption, "Young Girls Run So Others Won't Have To."

Several years ago, I taught 5-year-olds in kindergarten. Many of the children attended a summer day-care program at the same school. Although I did not teach in the summer, I brought junior high girls to be with the children, read them Bible stories, and led them in arts and crafts.

After having battled breast cancer, I encouraged the girls to get involved in the Hope Lodge, a facility where cancer patients can stay free of charge while receiving treatment. One grade from the ministry goes each week to visit with the guests. The girls make posters with Bible verses to tape on everybody's door. They plan theme parties such as Hawaiian Bingo, Make Your Own Sundaes, and Easter

Egg Dyeing. The patients and the girls are able to get to know each other and share prayer requests and encouragement.

The girls have found ministry opportunities especially suited to them in so many different places: nursing homes, retirement homes, girls clubs, an orphanage, a center for children with cerebral palsy, the local Children's Hospital. When we visit places like these during a holiday, the girls usually take something to give. Flowers, candy, cards, and posters make the initial approach easier.

We also look for disasters and the resulting needs we can meet. Once, a plastic surgeon mentioned to me that he was flying to Honduras to work with people in a particular village. A hurricane had heavily damaged the area and a cholera epidemic had broken out. The people were without food and clothes. I mentioned this to the girls, who mentioned it to one of their teachers. He announced it over the public address system at the school and before we knew it, the surgeon had to charter a boat to take all the supplies to Honduras that students had contributed.

We've sent literally thousands of cards and notes to sick children over the years, as well as posters with everyone's signature to people who are discouraged, disabled, or need to be congratulated. The girls have collected and sent books to an orphanage in South America and toys to a child dying of cancer in Oregon.

Amy came home from a vacation to find that her home had been completely destroyed by fire. Her club quickly developed a plan. Every girl brought clothes, jewelry, makeup . . . anything they thought she might like. They did not bring their leftovers. As a group, the girls then collected money and bought a Bible, and each inscribed her signature inside. Everyone came over for dinner. They spread out the clothes according to outfits, with matching accessories included. I'll never forget the look on Amy's face when she walked in the room. She was so excited that her friends had done this for her.

The blessings from serving others flow both ways. People we have served in turn serve us. Residents at the nursing homes we visit started having candy to give to the girls when we come. The kindergarten children colored pictures for the girls.

Mrs. Mabry was one of the girls' favorite people. She was 91 years old, very crippled, and lived in a little room at the retirement community. She always appeared eager to see the girls and would cover her bed with stuffed animals for them to play with each time they came to visit. One hot summer day, the girls arrived, flowers and cards in hand, ready to visit and sing. Immediately, they started for Mrs. Mabry's room. An orderly turned us back and led us to a huge living room. Privately, I was told that one of the residents had just died. The ambulance was on the way. The girls began to ask why they had to stay in the room. "Can't we please wait in Mrs. Mabry's room?" they asked. Thinking this would be a wonderful idea, I mentioned it to a nurse. Her eyes locked on mine. She said nothing but I knew that it was Mrs. Mabry who had died.

The ambulance came and went. Mrs. Mabry's nurse walked into the room where we waited. "Girls, this morning Mrs. Mabry was so excited that you were coming to see her. She had dressed in her favorite outfit and had us comb her hair perfectly. She was placing all the animals on the bed for you when her heart gave out. Girls, she went to be with Jesus in no pain. She was just getting ready for you."

Tears began to flow as the girls realized their loss. The nurse gave each one a stuffed animal, prepared for them by Mrs. Mabry.

I knew we couldn't visit with any of the other residents

that day. We walked several blocks to a park that was nearby and sat down under the trees. We talked about life and death, about serving, about loving, and then losing. Everyone cried. The girls loved Mrs. Mabry.

The ice-cream truck drove by, and I bought everyone ice cream. Suddenly the sprinkler system in the park came on, and water began to spray everywhere. The girls immediately started running and jumping in the tremendous streams of water. They were laughing and screaming as their bodies became more and more soaked.

A reporter from one of the local daily newspapers drove by and then stopped. "What's going on?" he asked. This was not supposed to be happening in the middle of the day! We started talking and I told him about the events of the morning. As a result, he wrote a story for the paper about our day and included a picture of the girls, with water spraying in all directions: "Girls Receive Showers After Showering Blessings on Others." In the article, he told the story of the relationship between Mrs. Mabry and the girls.

"And do not forget to do good and to share with others, for with such sacrifices God is pleased" (Heb. 13:16).

Look around you. Opportunities for service, both big and small, are everywhere. Everyone can serve . . . even those being served.

8

Girls, Groups, Identity, and Belonging

8

Girls, Groups, Identity, and Belonging

Girls love to belong. And for the most part, they like to be in groups and close to each other, emotionally and physically. Just notice them the next time you are together. In a large room, they will choose to sit on one or two sofas instead of in individual chairs. At a sleepover, they will pile sleeping bags into one big room if it is available, rather than spread them out over several rooms. It's a "girl thing" that seems to know no age limit.

For many of the ideas I have implemented in our ministry's Bible studies, I must give credit to my college sorority. Over 100 girls from varied backgrounds, cities, and states came together in unity and sisterhood. I was loyal to the sorority then and still am. Even today, as I speak on various college campuses, I find that we are still "sisters." I still remember the handshake and many sorority secrets. In fact, to this day, I've never revealed a single secret that we were privileged to learn upon initiation.

As our first Bible study was beginning, so many ideas came to me as a result of my sorority experience. How do you take a group of girls and help this group bond and form its own identity? I didn't begin this ministry with a neatly laid plan. The first group just sort of happened; but by the time the second group was established, the sister-hood idea was being birthed.

When the initial group began, the girls wanted a club where they and their friends could learn how to walk, how to talk, how to put on makeup, and do other things young women need to learn how to do. I had recently resigned as a flight attendant with a major American airline, and the girls loved to browse through my training school notebook that covered everything you ever wanted to know about personal appearance, poise, and good manners. But I knew that since the church would be supporting this ministry, the club should be more than just a charm course. So the girls and I compromised. We studied different women characters in the Bible each week, and afterwards worked on good grooming and etiquette. Because it was summer, this first group wore their swimsuits and brought their lunch along with their Bibles and notebooks.

Our Bible studies have always met in homes. Many gracious families throughout the years have let us use their playrooms, living rooms, family rooms, backyards, swim-ming pools, and porches. And because girls represent so many different denominations, it seems best not to meet at a particular church.

At one of those typical early meetings, the girls jumped into the swimming pool first. And since not everyone arrived at exactly the same time, I had ample time as leader to speak with each girl individually and get an idea of where she was emotionally that day. The time in the pool gave the girls a perfect opportunity to interact with each other and allowed them to get to know new girls as they joined the group. After the girls swam, we spread beach towels on the grass under big shade trees and ate lunch.

Bible study, about 30 minutes in length, followed this.

After the Bible study, we participated in some activities related to personal appearance to help the girls learn how to develop into godly young women. Because this first Bible study began during the hippie era, parents were delighted that their daughters wanted to look their best. The girls actually practiced walking, sitting, standing, and moving about in a graceful manner. They learned how to give manicures and pedicures. You can imagine how they loved putting nail polish on each other! A local department store brought clothing to show the girls how to build their wardrobes and mix and match appropriately for all occasions. A skin-care expert taught them how to take care of their complexion and a beautician worked with each girl to see just which hairstyle was most becoming for her. It was fun! Everyone had a great time, and little by little these young girls grew into beautiful, gracious young women.

That first Bible study group grew from 12 to over 60 in a 3-month period. Anita, the girl who first approached me about beginning it, and I talked at the very beginning about the fact that no one would ever be turned away. We wanted every girl to feel welcomed and included.

Singing has always been a part of these Bible study groups. Several of the girls in that first group played guitar and brought them to the meetings each week. Once a month we piled into cars for our service project, which involved singing for the residents at various nursing homes. The girls made cards and took flowers and candy as they visited up and down the halls with the residents. Afterwards we would go to lunch at a nice restaurant and practice good manners and proper etiquette. Although it sounds almost obsolete today, the girls then would always wear "Sunday" dresses. They loved every part of these days. They were proud of how they looked and what they did.

This first Bible study group continued to grow for 2 years before a new one began. I had decided to earn a master's degree in Christian education. Since the classes met at night and on weekends, I could work during the day and still have time to meet the girls for Bible study at Anita's house each week.

When I finished my master's degree, I accepted a position as Bible teacher in a Christian school. My homeroom was a 7th-grade class. Immediately the girls in that grade began to beg me to start a Bible study club for them. Even with having Bible class every day in school, they wanted a club of their own. I thought this was a wonderful idea and gave my OK. I was not prepared for the reaction of the girls in the original Bible study group. Tears, tears, and more tears! "You won't have time for us anymore," they wailed.

"Wait a minute! I need your help!" I explained. "I want you to be the big sisters of the girls in this new group." Immediately gloom broke out into smiles. They loved the idea and it worked for many years.

I worked carefully to match older girls with younger ones, trying to bring together similarities as well as differences in personalities that helped strengthen relationships as they developed. I considered personal interests, family dynamics, and even size. It would not have worked well for a little sister to tower over the big sister in height. The older girl needed to feel and look older.

Each week the big sister/little sister pairs wrote notes, made cards, or brought candy to give to each other. We spread out everything on a table at the meeting, and that was the first place everyone looked as the girls came into Bible study. This was even more exciting than refreshments after a long day at school. I enjoyed watching them tear open the notes and begin reading. These relationships helped the older girls feel responsible for another person and the younger girls to feel accepted. For the most part, this concept worked very well. The only problems arose when girls didn't reach out to their sisters. Usually if the older girl took a strong lead, the younger would follow. As the leader, I tried to watch for those girls who might be left out and get their feelings hurt.

As a new Bible study was formed each year, the line of big and little sisters continued. Many girls could list the "family" line without fault. This continued for many "generations," but eventually the program grew so large, and new girls constantly joined, so that there was no way to keep up with everyone. The big sister/little sister concept works well with smaller groups and requires that the leader urge the girls to keep notes and cards coming consistently.

Believe it or not, these Bible studies began before the T-shirt became popular among girls. The first groups wore dresses both to school and to Bible study. I remember giving everyone ribbons alike to wear in their long flowing hair. But as times changed, the girls began to ask, "Could we please have Bible study T-shirts?" I agreed.

At first, each Bible study club had its own distinct shirt. Girls in each group voted on color as well as design. By this time there were four clubs, and they chose the colors pink, light blue, yellow, and purple. The front of each shirt featured our Bible study logo, but the backs featured different designs for each club, drawn by the girls themselves. Also on the shirt's back each girl had her own signature plus the signatures of all the other club members.

As both the number of girls and the number of clubs increased, we chose one T-shirt pattern for the fall and another for the spring. The girls also had the opportunity to order a variety of other identity items such as long-sleeved T-shirts, sweatshirts, fleece jackets, vests, and blankets for the fall; and short-sleeved T-shirts, shorts, nightshirts, boxers, and beach towels for the spring. Year-round the girls could buy binders, pens, tote bags, laundry bags, pillowcases, visors, even shoestrings—all of which featured our logo.

The girls wore their T-shirts to service projects, Bible study, and school. Everyone knew who they were and what they represented. The wonderful thing was the fact that any girl who wanted to be a part of the group was encouraged to join.

I watched a pattern develop. As soon as a new girl moved to the area, girls in the Bible study immediately invited her to become a part of their group. School guidance counselors and principals began to contact me about new girls they felt would benefit from being a part of Bible study.

The mother of one 7th-grader, new to the school and the group, once wrote me, "As I see Jennifer getting ready for her Atlanta trip, I am thanking our Lord for a truly answered prayer. . . . My constant prayer has been that she find a Christian friend and that God would lead her to this friend—and there you are leading her to a special group. Thank you so much for all you do and for helping my daughter find her place of new friends. I am appreciative and forever grateful. Have a wonderful time and we shall pray for a safe and happy, fun trip."

As the Bible studies of this ministry grew, they crossed not only denominational lines but also schools and different parts of town. Girls who were homeschooled began to attend, some who lived as much as an hour away. Eventually the ministry and groups grew so that a girl could now begin with Bible study group when she started the 5th grade and continue until she graduated from high school.

In the midst of the program's tremendous growth, the sisterhood stayed strong. Eventually we moved from the big sister/little sister concept to a leadership team where older girls were in charge of as many as 10 younger girls. Those who did not choose to be leaders in this way could participate in leading parts of the meetings. Other older girls served as chaperons and counselors for the younger girls on retreats and trips. Some volunteered to plan games or do artwork. Everyone could find her place.

Each Bible study group elected officers, including president, a vice-president from each school, secretary, and a treasurer from each school. Groups also formed committees with a chairman and cochairman in areas such as social, service, refreshments, prayer, missions, and encouragement. As a result, every girl had a job and the clubs functioned as a body.

As it has evolved and grown, the ministry has become more of a commitment for girls entering high school. Their groups focus on discipleship. Older girls who are in college, out of college, married, and single volunteer as leaders and speakers in these high school groups. The sisterhood continues and has now come full circle. Women who were in the first Bible study groups now have daughters in various groups.

Carol, who was in the very first Bible study group and who now has a daughter in a group, wrote, "My memories of Bible study are filled with happy times, great friends, nursing home visits, long marathon summer days with swimming and lunch, trips to Atlanta, trips to Florida, lots of singing with the guitars, dressing up for lunch at fancy restaurants, practicing our manners. . . . I am happy Allison will experience all these fun things and probably more. But as I think of what you [Donna] have done for me personally, this is what I am excited about for Allison to be a part of.

"Donna, you gave us much more than a Bible lesson," she continued. "You not only taught us the Scriptures, but gave us a relationship! The way God wants you to treat others was 'taught' in a lesson but 'caught' as we all worked on service projects together. You taught us the biblical principles of friendship. More importantly you encouraged us to reach out to new girls, make everyone feel welcome, and make new friends. Thank you for building our self-confidence. How many times have you said to us, 'You are what you are becoming'? My prayer is that Allison sees Jesus in Donna just like her mamma did!"

Allison, her daughter and the first second-generation Bible study girl, wrote, "The first time I went to Donna's Bible study I felt nervous. I looked around and there were a lot of people I didn't know. It seemed like forever until my friends arrived. Donna is terrific. She just finished teaching us about cliques and being a clique breaker. Now we are studying the Book of James. Donna tells great stories and I like Bible study a lot. Now we are just waiting for our new Bible study T-shirts."

Community Ministry for Girls is now deeply entrenched in our community. The roots grow deeply and are layered in relationships of spiritual bonds. Over 3,000 girls have been a part of the program to date, and the harvest is now in full bounty with a ripple effect of blessings to follow. "Still other seed fell on good soil. It came up and yielded a crop, a hundred times more than was sown" (Luke 8:8). Girls have moved across the country and have started clubs of their own. Many have married ministers or become missionaries. The girls are literally in the four corners of the earth.

It doesn't take a lot to get a group or club like this started. The leader is key. She should love God, love girls, and strive toward the criteria described in chapter 3. She is instrumental in determining what the girls will learn and how. Christian bookstores offer a variety of workbooks and

Bible studies, but many leaders like to plan their own. This has always worked best for me. I also make work sheets for the girls to use as I teach, and I provide notebooks for them to keep these work sheets organized. The girls also receive Bible verse assignments each week to memorize. And at some point we developed a songbook, and the girls added this to their notebooks. There is probably no limit to the extras you can include, but the most important element is the mentor relationship that helps girls make the transition from adolescence to adulthood.

"I planted the seed, Apollos watered it, but God made it grow. So neither he who plants nor he who waters is anything, but only God, who makes things grow" (1 Cor. 3:6–7).

9

The Importance of Rewards

The Importance of Rewards

I still have the very yellow piece of paper. My daddy was in pharmacy school. My mother was in the delivery room. Daddy studied as I was being born. The doctor came to the waiting room to pronounce the good news. "Mr. Greene, it's a girl!"

As Mother recovered, Daddy wrote, "February 11, 8:47 A.M. Baby Donna Margaret is born. Goals for her life: By the time she is able to speak she'll memorize Scripture—to be paid by the verse." And so I grew up memorizing Scripture. For every verse I memorized, I earned a nickel. As I tell this story to the girls in our Bible study clubs, they often remark, "A nickel? I surely wouldn't do it for just that!" Well, times have changed, especially in the world of nickels. Five cents bought a soft drink when I was growing up. And since my daddy was a pharmacist and worked in a drugstore, I had easy access to a soft-drink machine, which took nickels. I knew a soft drink would be waiting for me for each verse I committed to my heart. My parents used this system of rewards for me and it worked well.

Gramma rewarded me in other ways. As I memorized passages of Scripture, she gave me satin pillowcases, pieces of china, and embroidered tablecloths and napkins. I put everything into a hope chest, not to be touched, but I enjoyed looking at those beautiful things and knew that they were there.

As a child I loved choosing stickers to put on my school papers when I made an A and watching my piano pieces be marked with stars and checks as I memorized a song.

Rewards are good. They mark a passage. Sometimes they are just the encouragement a person needs to keep going. I still find it exciting to cross the finish line of a marathon and have a medal placed around my neck. The medal itself is not very valuable, but you can't put a price on what it represents.

And so our Bible studies are filled with a series of rewards. The younger girls put stickers by their names for attendance and for memorizing Bible verses. Perfect attendance or memory work earns a greater reward at the end of the year.

Sixth-grade girls memorize Proverbs 31. Each girl who does so receives a silver cross, engraved with *Proverbs 31* on one side and her initials on the other side. Seventh-grade girls are challenged to memorize 50 Bible verses and are rewarded with a trip to Atlanta.

Retreats, trips, and overnights are important rewards of Bible study clubs. Trips to the beach, the lake, farms and plantations, wherever we go, our purpose is to build relationships with God and each other. Girls love to be close to each other and these concentrated times help to facilitate this. These can be as simple or elaborate as the leader wants them to be. Trips to Atlanta are favorites of the girls in Birmingham. A bus awaits them as they meet early on a Saturday morning. They play games the entire way over that cause them to mix and get to know each other better. Arriving around noon, the girls go to a huge mall where they eat lunch and shop for spring clothes, especially bathing suits. We designate specific times for the group to meet back together during the day. Each meeting has a purpose—a game, a scavenger hunt—anything to make them more comfortable with each other. Then it's on to the hotel. I assign the rooms, placing high school girls with the younger ones. The girls never have a choice as to who will be in their rooms. This way no one feels the pressure of being left out. Free time follows as they swim, work out, or just hang out with each other.

Sometimes we go out to dinner. Other times the girls prefer a pizza party at the hotel. After that the real fun begins with a fashion show in one of the hotel conference rooms. Each girl models what she bought (or didn't buy!). I remember one 7th-grade girl walking across the stage with money taped all over her clothes. Her comment: "This is the money that I saved today." Many girls buy the same outfit or shoes and model them together, accompanied by music and commentary. They really get into it. A talent show follows and then the mood changes.

The girls go to their rooms, change into their pajamas, and return to the conference room. We clear the room of remnants of the fashion and talent shows and turn our attention to praise music, testimonies, Bible readings, and prayer for the next two to three hours. Following this, girls share more intimately in their rooms with their high school leaders.

The next morning we meet together for worship. The girls and their leaders are responsible for this, and each set of roommates takes a turn. We have music and prayer, followed by lunch, and then we board the bus to return home. I usually put a movie in the VCR and most of the girls sleep all the way home. Friendships are always made and renewed, and it's always a successful trip.

Dear Donna,
Thank you so much for having Bible study every year! This year was so much fun! I had so much fun in Atlanta and at the lake. This year I felt like has been the best since I've been coming. Everyone really got to know each other and we all had a great time. I'm going to write you and get you to write me at camp. I hope I get to see you this summer and maybe get together. I'm really looking forward to being in Bible study next year.
—from a 13-year-old

As the girls enter high school, they can enjoy longer trips. Over an 8-year period they are able to fill their scrapbooks and memories with monumental treasures from their time in Bible study groups with their friends. It is something that will always be a part of their lives.

Thank you so much for taking us to the beach. Once again you have been so giving of your time. It was a wonderful trip with lots of sharing times and memories that will last a lifetime. Donna, I thank you so much for everything you've done for me. You play such a huge role in my life and have for 7 years. I love spending time with you. Thanks again and I hope to see you soon.
—from a 16-year-old

"Only be careful, and watch yourselves closely so that you do not forget the things your eyes have seen or let them slip from your heart as long as you live. Teach them to your children and to their children after them" *(Deut. 4:9).*

10

Developing Effective Bible Studies

10

Developing Effective Bible Studies

It is Monday after Bible study, after that wonderful lesson on giving. That lesson inspired me so much that I came home, gave all my money to the church, filled two garbage bags full of clothes, toys, games, shoes, socks—things I always wanted to hold on to, but, through the lesson God was telling me to let it all go—to someone who really needed it! I am filled with the very best feeling I have ever felt! Giving and giving cheerfully with God. And now I just can't wait for God to give me something so I can give again! I absolutely love Bible study! It has done so much for my life and I have grown so much closer to the Lord.

—from a 13-year-old

Donna, I felt that I needed to write this letter to thank you for helping me become a Christian. I learn so much in Bible study that I want to pass the word along. It was not until this year that I became a true Christian and I am grateful for my faith every day. Donna, I used to cry a lot and since Jesus has been in my heart, I only cry for joy and the peace I have within myself. I have a best friend that is unsure about her faith right

now. So every night I spend about an hour on the phone teaching her about Jesus and helping her figure out that she wants to become a Christian. Tonight, as we were talking she read me a letter that she wrote to God asking Him to come into her heart. Instantly a smile came upon my face and I thanked the Lord. For it was Him who changed me and I hope that I might be able to make a difference. My father has not led the perfect lifestyle due to problems in the past. I feel that God is bringing me closer to my dad in hopes that one day I might make a difference in him. This summer I am going to live with him. It will be then I will counsel him and spread the Christian faith. I will start out with the question, "If you die tomorrow, where will you spend eternity?" I think that I have all the power through God to change my dad and help him become a Christian. I know I still have a lot to learn but your influence on me has changed my life for the better. The smile you see on my face every day is my heart smiling and it has all the reason to because Christ is in it. I look up to you so much in that you are so brave and wise to teach me and many other girls what being a Christian is all about. You have changed my life and I thank you!
        —from a 14-year-old

These two letters didn't come immediately after I taught my very first Bible study. In fact, after teaching that first time, I knew I needed a lot of improvement. I had written down every single word and memorized the words from those typed sheets verbatim. It was sort of like reading from a book, except that I had committed the entire lesson to memory. I felt exhausted after that half hour. But amazingly, those girls came back the following week for more Bible study. Not only did they come back, they also brought friends and girls that no one knew. Many girls had heard about this club and wanted to be a part of it.

One particular seminary course, Teaching the Book of Galatians, taught me how to teach. Frank M. Barker, the chancellor of Birmingham Theological Seminary, taught our class how to take a book of the Bible and develop lessons from it, taking into consideration the personality and spiritual maturity of the group. God uses faithful people who are willing. He takes us where we are and helps us become what we can be. Part of that process includes training and exposing us to teachers who have gone before us. Following are some of the lessons I learned from others about how to teach God's Word.

Some Guidelines for Teachers, Teaching, and Learning

- •A teacher must personally and thoroughly know the lesson or truth he or she is teaching.
- •Teachers and students must communicate in a language that is common to both. Teachers should use words, illustrations, and language students can clearly understand.
- •Teachers should aim to keep students' minds in an attitude of discovery and anticipation, which leads to action. Learning can't happen effectively when students are disinterested.
- •Teachers should begin with what students already know well—with what they have experienced for themselves. Teachers should illuminate new truths in light of truths students already know. What is unknown must be explained by what is known.
- •Teachers should help students reproduce new truths in their own language. Real teaching and learning happen when a student's mind grasps the desired truth and integrates it into his or her own understanding.

•Review is essential, as new truths grow deeper with added meanings and applications.

Asking questions is one of the most powerful methods of stimulating, deepening, or changing the direction of a lesson. The leader of a Bible study will be effective to the degree and depth of her questions. Ask good questions that stimulate thoughts, which in turn allow for great discussions. Good questions are neither leading nor limiting; instead, they are open; in fact, wide open.

This is not always possible in a very large group setting. Utter chaos can erupt if 100 girls are allowed to interject their thoughts simultaneously. But in smaller Bible study groups or in small groups that break out from a large group for discussion, this works well.

Many resources are available in Christian bookstores to help you prepare Bible studies. Lessons can be developed from many different angles. Some leaders like to teach from workbooks or lessons that have already been prepared. Others like to write their own; in this case, Bible commentaries and concordances can help you develop studies especially suited for your group.

Developing and Evaluating Teaching Skills

Teaching abilities and skills do not usually happen overnight. Most teachers must develop and refine them over time. I memorized every word of the first Bible lesson I taught. Now after nearly 30 years of teaching, I rarely look at my notes. Bible study leaders and teachers should regularly take inventory of their teaching experiences and watch for opportunities for improvement. Use the following questions to evaluate your ability to lead and guide your group in Bible study.

•Do I lead, or do I allow the group to lead me?

•Do I listen?

•Am I sensitive to the needs of the group?

•Do I easily get off course? Are there ever any tangents? How do these usually occur? How can I best avoid them or deal with them?

•Do I follow a plan closely? Why or why not?

•Do I prepare adequately? If not, what do I need to do differently?

•What have I learned that I can include in future planning?

•Do I carefully interpret and apply the Scriptures?

•Do I adequately cover the biblical material? Do I stay on the subject? If not, why?

•Is each student motivated to contribute her best during the study? What do I need to do to ensure that this will happen each time?

•Are the practical applications of biblical truths in keeping with the truths of the Scriptures?

•Are the applications specific and practical?

•What do I do to encourage students to carry out applications from previous Bible study discussions?

•How well do group members know each other?

•How well do group members listen to each other?

Guiding Groups Toward Unity of Purpose

Adequate and effective group discussion happens when individuals feel comfortable expressing ideas and share relationships with each other. Most people feel uncomfortable opening up to a group of strangers. Part of your role as a mentor, leader, and teacher is to facilitate group unity. Consider the following suggestions.

•Make sure that group members have opportunities to meet each other and learn everyone's name.

- As group leader, learn the name of every person in the group and use people's names frequently.
- After the first meeting, informally mix group members and reintroduce them in new ways.
- Know each girl well enough for her to place great confidence in you. When a girl identifies with the leader, she has more confidence in herself and is more willing to speak. She will also be more open to the leader's correction and discipline when these are necessary.

"Be shepherds of God's flock that is under your care, serving as overseers—not because you must, but because you are willing, as God wants you to be; not greedy for money, but eager to serve; not lording it over those entrusted to you, but being examples to the flock" (1 Peter 5:2–3).

Becoming a good teacher is a process. Don't give in to discouragement if a discussion goes wrong or doesn't meet your expectations. Recognize mistakes and use them to find new ways to improve your ability to lead Bible study. This is part of the learning process. God is honored when His word goes forth. God is a God of encouragement. Discouragement can always be traced to Satan. Continue to seek the Lord, asking for His wisdom and guidance in leading those He has placed under your care.

"We do not dare to classify or compare ourselves with some who commend themselves. When they measure themselves by themselves and compare themselves with themselves, they are not wise" (2 Cor. 10:12).

The Bible warns us not to compare ourselves to others. Every person is unique with special abilities that need to be developed.

Most importantly, don't give up! Stick with the group if you know for certain it is the will of God. Follow the goal to completion. Every leader must start where she is, and where her group is. The world is changed one life at a time. A teacher will only know her realm of influence in eternity: "'The one who received the seed that fell on good soil is the man who hears the word and understands it. He produces a crop, yielding a hundred, sixty or thirty times what was sown'" (Matt. 13:23).

11

Using Stories to Teach

11

Using Stories to Teach

I love stories. I remember stories. I look at life as a series of stories. As a child, I can remember writing stories in my head even when I wasn't in the position to write them on paper. Being bored was never an option for me. If one of my teachers began to cover material I was already familiar with, I tuned her out and let my mind create whatever it wanted to. My daddy was a storyteller, so I grew up listening, creating, and seeing the world around me and inside me as a paradise of adventures in story form.

Throughout the years in our ministry, I have heard girls say countless times, "Donna, tell us a story!" My response is usually, "What category?" And they always proceed with their requests. My stories are usually my own because it's hard to remember what happens to someone else, at least for very long. But I can remember the details of my life—not only the facts but also the emotions.

I've worked in some way with children since I was 13 years old. My experience has been varied—orphanage, children's hospital, clinic for children with disabilities, kindergarten, school, Girls Club, Head Start program. I've always found that just the right story at just the right moment can alter most any situation that arises. An appropriate story can change moods, even when circumstances can't be changed.

Every child I've ever worked with has loved to listen to story after story. I can't even count the number of story marathons during a spend-the-night party or drive to or from the beach with girls from the Bible study group. Stories can entertain, teach, inspire, admonish, and reinforce. Stories solidify images that reinforce Bible truths. They paint pictures of reality and bring new life to old points.

Jesus taught with stories. His parables are illustrations of moral lessons. He knew how much easier it is for people to recall important truths by remembering a story that illustrates that truth.

Everyone has personal stories to tell. Perhaps these examples from my experiences, which I now use as I lead Bible studies, will illustrate how you can weave storytelling into your own Bible studies.

Many years ago I went with a church youth group for a weekend at the beach. We were to leave at 4:00 on a Friday afternoon, spend Saturday at the beach, help with a church service on Sunday morning, and then return home that evening. Everyone arrived at the appointed time, excited and ready to go. As we approached Montgomery, we found ourselves in the middle of a terrible storm. In fact, all the power was out in the city. Our plan had been to stop there for dinner; but, of course, that plan failed since none of the restaurants had electricity. I noticed that the fuel gauge was almost on empty and filled up the tank at that time.

We drove on to Dothan, and once again I noticed that the fuel was low. I was driving the station wagon of one of the girl's parents—not my own car. "Maybe it's just a gas guzzler," I thought. We drove on toward Florida. We were in a caravan of four vehicles. As we traveled through country back roads, windows down on a beautiful spring night, the girls' feet propped high and heads leaned back, one gently remarked, "Oh, Donna, look at all the pretty lightning bugs!" Another chaperon, Al, was by this time driving, and I was seated in the front passenger seat. I peered out the windows to see little orange streams of flickering light. It really was beautiful. "Is it phosphorus?" I wondered. I rolled down the window further and immediately smelled smoke.

"Al! Quick! Pull the car over and signal the others," I said. Our signal was flashing lights and beeping horns. As soon as the car stopped, I jumped out, ran toward the hood of the car, and saw immediately that the entire engine was on fire. Having been a flight attendant, my emergency procedure mode kicked right in. Throwing open the back doors of the car, I began to pull the girls out, telling them to run across to the other side of the road. Al and I pulled out as much luggage from the back as possible before the flames hit the front seat. Then we had to run, as explosions sent streams of fire and smoke into the night air.

The other vehicles in our group returned to where we were, and we all watched with amazement as the station wagon completely burned up. It was a true adventure—much like a television or movie scene.

What lessons did we learn?

The girls were frightened and crying. We were in the middle of nowhere, and it was pitch black. Most of their shoes and purses had burned up. No one thought to grab these items in the very quick evacuation. It was an awesome sight to watch. Almost immediately, I called everyone together and said, "Girls, you are ruining a perfectly good adventure by being upset. There is nothing we can do to keep that car from burning. You may never see anything like this again in your entire life. Now settle down and enjoy it!"

Next thing I knew, they were all on the rooftops of the other vehicles singing, "It only takes a spark to get a car burning." Their moods had completely changed.

This was well before the days of car phones and cell phones. We sat for a long time as other motorists slowed down, took a long look, and then moved on. No one stopped to help us. Hours passed; then a couple of obviously very poor men pulled over and offered assistance. They were the ones who notified the highway patrol.

It was dawn as we pulled back into the church parking lot. To their delight, the girls had been driven to the beach by a sheriff in his patrol car. Laura remembered, "Oh Donna, I brought marshmallows for us to roast."

"Don't worry, Laura. They were roasted!"

The lesson? We made the most of a bad situation. The girls saw a living example of a good Samaritan.

When I was a flight attendant and living in New York City, I decided to spend one of my days off shopping. Macy's on 34th Street was my store of choice that day. I needed hosiery, and at that time items like that were stored behind the counter. As I waited for the clerk to help me, I listened as she became very aggravated with another customer. I walked away and went downstairs to the pharmacy where I purchased a small tin of aspirin and a soft drink before returning to the hosiery counter. By this time, the clerk was alone. Placing the soft drink and aspirin in front of her I remarked, "It must be hard to work in New York City. I thought this might help." She literally fell backwards onto a stool.

"Well, I've never had anyone do something for me," she replied.

We started to talk. Over time, we became friends. Much later she asked Christ to come into her heart.

The lesson? You never know when a chance encounter will result in a new friendship and the opportunity to tell someone else about Christ.

During college, I spent two summers as housemother for 10 little girls who had been taken from their parents due to abusive situations. They shared one big room in the children's home, with five beds lining one wall and five more lining the opposite wall. The morning I arrived, apprehension filled the room. They were shy, nervous, and timid. "Who is this new person?" they wondered.

From my first moment with them, I decided to make this room of girls into a family, at least for the summer. What a tiring, yet extremely rewarding, experience.

Morning came after a somewhat fitful first night's sleep. I awoke to find 10 wet beds, and 10 little heads hung low. This was going to be a family affair, I explained. Everyone was to help each other. Surrounding the beds one by one, 5 girls on one side and 5 on the other, we systematically stripped and remade each bed. By the end of summer all beds stayed dry.

The lesson? God's love in and through us can do amazing things and can fill others with security and confidence like they've never known.

One time during one of our Bible studies we were talking about temptation. A 5th-grade girl raised her hand and said, "I have a story. My mother has a cookie jar in our kitchen. She bakes homemade cookies for us once a week and that keeps the jar full. It's for us, but we're not allowed to eat any without permission. One night I went downstairs to get something to drink. Everyone was asleep, or so I thought. Seeing the kitchen light on, I quietly tiptoed in. There stood my younger brother, hand reaching toward that cookie jar. He didn't know that I was there, so I stood really still. The hand finally came down as he continued to stand. Once again, that hand came up, this time actually touching the jar. He stood for several minutes before slapping his own hand and saying, 'Nice try, Devil!'"

The lesson? God always gives us a way out of temptation.

Charlie L. Chops, or Charlie Lamb Chops as we called him, was my solid-white, part-Persian cat. He had been left as a very tiny kitten on a shelf in my daddy's drugstore. When he brought Charlie home in his coat pocket, Daddy became the rescuer and hero of the day. Charlie Chops made his home with me for the next 11 years.

Charlie had it made. He slept on my pillow beside me every night. He had all the food he wanted and a place to keep dry, cool, or warm. He even had his own cat door. But Charlie wasn't satisfied.

In the den was a huge aquarium filled with fish of every size, shape, and color. Charlie loved to watch those fish and would sit for hours, his head moving up and down and side to side with each movement of the fish. A lid fit snugly on the aquarium to protect the fish, with a light bulb attached beneath it to keep them warm.

Charlie always woke me up in the morning by playing with my face or chewing on my hair. It was impossible to sleep late, but somehow that Saturday I did. Charlie wasn't there.

As I went downstairs I called to him. Nothing. And then I saw . . . poor, poor Charlie. There he was in that aquarium, half the water on the floor with dead fish everywhere. The few that managed to stay alive swam slowly around the sopping wet Charlie. Apparently the lid had been left open, but now it was shut. Without my help, Charlie was stuck.

Every day Charlie had looked lovingly at that fish bowl. Now he had his wish, but it wasn't at all what he thought it would be. I imagined those fish had been looking at Charlie and thinking, "No fair! That fat cat gets to sleep on a soft sofa all day long and go wherever he wants, while we have to stay in this one bowl." For Charlie the desire led to misery. For the fish the desire led to death.

The lesson? God's plan is good. He wants only what is best for us and will give it to us as we walk in the path He designs for us.

These are just a few examples of the hundreds of stories I have in my story bank. I don't plan stories; they just come up. Life is full of stories. Some seem to be classics, and the girls request them over and over. But many take place during the week of the Bible study, or even that very day.

How can you build your own story bank?

•Pay attention to what goes on around you. Stories are everywhere!

•Become aware of truths that your students need to know. Try to attach stories to these truths.

•If personal storytelling is not your gift, look for stories from books, articles, and the Internet. (Remember, though, not all stories found on the Internet are true.)

•Think of ways your students can transfer these truths to their lives and into their experiences.

•Practice telling stories out loud.

•Keep on practicing!

One girl in reflecting on her years in Bible study said to me, "I've decided that my life is every bit as interesting as yours is. You just know how to tell it better."

Whenever I sense I'm losing the interest of the group or they've been sitting too long, I stop and quietly say, "Oh! That reminds me of a story."

All eyes are now on me and they wait in anticipation.

12

Teaching Through Activities

12

Teaching Through Activities

A camp in Etna, California, offers high school students a wonderful two-week Christian leadership program called Second Wind. Students who leave are never again the same. The lessons they learn become an integral part of their lives. The camp's motto, from Bruce Johnston, explains why: I Heard, and I Forgot. I Saw, and I Remembered. I Did, and I Understood.

Students at the camp are placed in real-life situations that allow them to put basic principles of life into action. Once they experience these practical applications, they own the teachings for themselves. They understand and their lives are forever changed.

Activities reinforce important life lessons and biblical truths and can be as varied and creative as the leader wants them to be. The following stories illustrate how I learned some very important life lessons from one of my most cherished mentors, my grandmother.

One summer when I was about 10 years old, Gramma decided to teach me about the godly woman Proverbs 31 describes. We read the chapter from the Bible and then separated the verses into categories. I still vividly remember the lessons I learned from Gramma because of the activities she used to teach me.

"She selects wool and flax and works with eager hands" *(Prov. 31:13).*

Gramma was so creative. Having survived the depression years, she knew how to save and be frugal. She was extremely neat and never wasted anything. She planned well, worked hard, and was extremely organized. I remember this verse because once Gramma had gotten a book of fabric scraps from a company that made men's suits. The book had numerous squares of various wool fabrics from which men could choose to have their suits custom made. Gramma took the squares and made them into a quilt. There were holes in the corners of each square, but that didn't bother her. She embroidered flowers around the holes, allowing each hole to become the center of a flower.

"She is like the merchant ships, bringing her food from afar" (Prov. 31:14).

There were no ships around where we lived, but Gramma often took me across town early in the morning to the farmer's market. Grampa would drive, as Gramma never got her driver's license until after he died. We would choose from many varieties of vegetables and fruits. Then it was home again to start preparing the food for freezing and canning. This was an all-day event, but by night we would have dozens of filled jars lining the counters, tightly sealed and in orderly rows. Later Gramma would store them in high cabinets that reached to the ceiling. All winter long we had plenty of vegetables and fruit preserves to eat. We could have whatever we wanted, but were always reminded, "A lot of hard work produced these, so don't waste them."

"She gets up while it is still dark; she provides food for her family and portions for her servant girls" (Prov. 31:15).

I never remember waking and finding Gramma still asleep. She normally got up at 5:30 A.M. so she could take care of her flowers before the sun got too hot. Many mornings I would go to the kitchen to find Gramma making homemade biscuits, which we would enjoy with some of our fig preserves. She never let me buy a jar of jam or jelly from the store. "That's just not good," she would say.

"She considers a field and buys it; out of her earnings she plants a vineyard" (Prov. 31:16).

Gramma lived in the suburbs of Birmingham—not the country. But somehow she was able to keep a garden going. An alley separated the main house from six lots that she and Grampa used for growing flowers, vegetables, fruit, and pecan trees. Grampa also had a worm bed for fishing bait. They used what they needed, gave away plenty, and sold some. Three huge pecan trees stood between the main house and a garage apartment, and Gramma had us gather all those pecans. She sold them by the pound and gave the money to missions.

"She sets about her work vigorously; her arms are strong for the tasks" (Prov. 31:17).

Although she had help with her yard work, Gramma liked to work hard with hedge clippers and lawn mowers.

She put me to work raking leaves or sweeping the walks and steps. I didn't particularly like this verse but she would remind me that I was descended from strong Tennessee stock.

"She sees that her trading is profitable, and her lamp does not go out at night" (Prov. 31:18).

Gramma had an old kerosene lamp. When my brothers and I would spend the night with her, she would light it for us and tell us about her childhood. Gramma never went to bed before we did.

"In her hand she holds the distaff and grasps the spindle with her fingers" (Prov. 31:19).

I especially enjoyed this activity. Gramma had an old pedal sewing machine. It was not electric and required major leg action to push it up and down and make the needle and thread do their stitching. We didn't use new material. Instead, we made dresses and doll dresses out of feed sacks and old curtains. Sound like Maria in *The Sound of Music?* I proudly wore my feed-sack dress to play in . . . only at home.

"She opens her arms to the poor and extends her hands to the needy" (Prov. 31:20).

I can remember many times filling baskets with fruit, vegetables, and, of course, Gramma's homemade preserves. Grampa would drive as Gramma and I carried the food to people who were poor or sick. Sometimes we would visit an elderly relative who had a piano, and I would be required to play all of my recital pieces for her. On holidays we made extraspecial baskets to take to Annie. She had been Gramma's housekeeper but was well up in age by this time. Many times I remember taking Annie a plate of dinner after we had finished ours.

"When it snows, she has no fear for her household; for all of them are clothed in scarlet. She makes coverings for her bed; she is clothed in fine linen and purple" (Prov. 31:21–22).

It doesn't snow much in the South and rarely gets extremely cold. But Gramma brought these verses alive for me through her quilts, many made of pieces of cloth left over from my childhood school dresses.

"Her husband is respected at the city gate, where he takes his seat among the elders of the land" (Prov. 31:23).

I never saw Grampa go to work. At an early age, his hand got caught in the wringer of an old washing machine. As a result, he contracted tetanus, which caused him to have lockjaw. He was sick for a long time and almost died. Along with this, Grampa had a rare lung disease. He always had difficulty breathing and was confined to a sanatorium for tuberculosis at one time. My most vivid recollections are of him in his big, overstuffed chair, reading his Bible. He drove and walked very slowly. Gramma did most of the physical labor around the house, but I never once heard her complain or make reference to Grampa's disabilities. Together, they were involved in starting a mission church. Every Saturday we went to make sure the Sunday School room was in order for class the next day. Gramma taught young children, "beginners," as they were called then. Often she would show me a pew with a plaque on it in honor of Grampa. She showed such respect for him and pointed the honor to him rather than herself.

"She makes linen garments and sells them, and supplies the merchants with sashes. She is clothed with strength and dignity; she can laugh at the days to come" (Prov. 31:24–25).

Gramma never worked outside of the home but made her home work for her. Grampa had owned a lumber company at one time. Rather than lay his men off during the depression, he had them build a rather large house for his family. Many relatives found shelter there during hard times. Gramma and Grampa raised three children there. My mother and daddy were given the garage apartment to live in when I was born. The house served the family well. Then everyone moved on except Gramma and Grampa. When Grampa's health began to fail severely, they divided the main house into three apartments. They converted the basement into a huge bedroom with at least five beds in it for grandchildren to sleep in when we stayed overnight. Gramma and Grampa rented the garage apartment and two apartments in the house, leaving ample room for them in which to live and constantly entertain grandchildren.

"She speaks with wisdom, and faithful instruction is on her tongue. She watches over the affairs of her household and does not eat the bread of idleness" (Prov. 31:26–27).

Gramma was a teacher. She found lessons in everything. She taught us constantly. She didn't entertain her grandchildren just to pass time. Everything had a purpose. She taught us to work but made it seem like fun. We would sit for hours as she taught me to embroider or type on a manual typewriter, all the while telling me stories about growing up in Tennessee.

"Her children arise and call her blessed; her husband also, and he praises her: 'Many women do noble things, but you surpass them all.' Charm is deceptive, and beauty is fleeting; but a woman who fears the Lord is to be praised. Give her the reward she has earned, and let her works bring her praise at the city gate" (Prov. 31:28–31).

Gramma died of breast cancer at the age of 72. Somehow we never thought she would die. She was indeed clothed with strength. The cancer had spread and her body became weaker. Yet just a month before her death my first nephew was born. Gramma cooked a huge dinner and delivered it to my brother's home. That was the last big task she completed.

One evening I walked into her living room and found her doubled over in incredible pain. She instructed me to call my mother as well as an ambulance. The doctors told us that she would certainly die without an operation and would probably die on the operating table. She made the decision to have surgery. Without it her death would have been excruciatingly painful. I was crying and her concern was for me. After her body had been filled with morphine, she sent for me. "Don't worry, Donna. Your ole Gramma is not going to die in that operating room." She was right. The surgeon couldn't believe it, but she pulled through and lived for one more week. After that week we could all let her go.

Gramma was one of my mentors. I didn't realize it at the time, but she constantly taught me with activities and projects. I learned from her what it means to be a godly woman by watching her and being a part of her life. It's

been said that more of life is caught than taught. Almost
30 years have passed since her death, but I remember those
lessons Gramma taught me as though I learned them yesterday.

The godly woman is kind, honest, hardworking, indus-
trious, caring, and holy. Her character reflects her Master,
Jesus Christ.

Before Gramma died, she cleared out her entire house,
had given away what she could, and placed instructions on
the back of all furniture as to who would receive it.
Through tears I asked her why she was doing this. "I will
have no arguing over my things after I am gone," she
replied. I have the cover of Gramma's will. The opening
lines read:

> Only one life
>   will soon be passed.
> Only what's done for Christ
>   will last.

Reflections

Reflections

As I was writing this book on mentoring girls, I often reflected on those early days. I had no idea what God was going to do with my life and this ministry with girls at its beginning. I honestly didn't really know what I was doing. I did love the girls and enjoyed being with them. In essence, I practiced on and learned through being with them. They never seemed to mind. I can look back to those days and now add my own perspective and wisdom, which has come from 30 years of experience. But I wanted to hear from them, as you probably do. So I asked them: What did you learn? How has Bible study affected your life? What is your perspective, now that you have daughters of your own?

Following are some of their reflections.

There is no way I could ever begin to put into words the impact that my years in our girls' Bible study have had on my life. I have truly thanked God so many times for the privilege of being a part of something that has shaped my values, my goals, and my life for eternity. I appreciate so much the time that Donna poured into us and her goal of helping us to become well-rounded young ladies who loved the Lord, loved to study His Word, and strove to be all God wanted us to be. Through Donna's lessons and her life she taught us how to love each other, how to build deep and lasting friendships, how to reach out to others and make them feel special, how to have a true and personal relationship with Jesus Christ, and how to serve each other and our community.

During a time in life when you are trying to figure out who you are and the direction you want your life to go, there could have been no greater positive influence than Donna and our Bible study. She made our study fun and exciting and "cool." We truly were the "peer pressure" because Christianity was made so attractive.

—*Anita Barker Barnes*

Thank you for giving your life for girls so that those girls could have little girls who can learn the truth of God and grow up to have their own little girls and the truth can be passed on and a world can be different. Thank you most of all for laying down your life to make mine different.

—*Beth Huff Jordan*

I think I know what Donna must have felt when she met with us as preteens, as I now have a 10-year-old daughter and my heart is bursting with all I want to tell Caroline about the Lord. One of the greatest blessings in my life is having people live out this faith before my very eyes. I thank Donna for the godly heritage that my precious angel is inheriting because of her investment in me.

—*Carol Colquitt Godwin*

What an incredible blessing for me to watch my girls enjoy the blessings I had as a child. They will visit a nursing home and learn a merciful spirit. They will learn to reach out and include each and every girl. They will learn God's word and

make friends with girls their own age who are like-minded.
They will visit a cancer center and learn unselfishness. They
will know only two things last forever—the word of God and
souls of men.

—Carol Harris Riley

The friendships that I developed during my Bible study years
are still, 30 years later, some of my closest. We do not see each
other every day, but there is a bond among us that is stronger
than most friendships. It has been said that you can't make old
friends. We are old friends because of the foundation of friend-
ship and love given to us at Bible study. As I reflect on my
Caroline's teen years, I pray that she will be blessed with
friends as I was: friends who "stick closer than a brother," who
will be there for her in many years and who love the Lord as
she does.

—Emily Snuggs Neel

Connections were made 30 years ago when a group of young
girls gathered for the first time in kneesocks, braces, and Mary
Jane shoes. We came to hear about makeup, boys, and Donna's
exciting life as a stewardess. She came to teach us what God
had to say about becoming young women. As we gathered year
after year, we forged connections that would extend to our
parents and our children and would prove to last a lifetime.
These connections are forged from a common past, a common
God, and a woman who took a keen interest in a group of
awkward young girls.

—Tracy Wheeler Jones

You invested so much in my life and I appreciate you. The foundation laid in my life is still paying dividends today. Your ministry is a testimony to the value of mentoring girls. I'm trusting God to raise up mentors for my own girls, much the same way God raised you up for me.
—Leila Welch Brazeal

Years have passed since that first meeting and I continue to remain close friends with those I giggled, cried, and prayed with each week. What a true blessing those years were in my life and I hope that I will be an instrument in others' lives as Donna was in mine. My prayer for my daughter, Marylane, is that she will be able to experience friendships, laughter, tears, and the joy of Christ's love as I was privileged to at such a young age.
—Lynn Haskew Graham

I cannot imagine what my life would be like had God not put me under Donna's mentorship. My fondest childhood memories are of that group of girls, gathered together and taught to love, taught to sing, and taught to live. We were taught how to grow into being young women and, more specifically, young Christian women. This was not done through lectures and studies alone but by genuine investment by Donna through her love for the Lord, her love for life, and her love for us. She gave us all confidence, not in ourselves, but in our Savior, and showed us how to take advantage of that confidence and let Jesus work through us for His glory.
—Holly Harrison Moore

When reflecting on my childhood years, my times with Donna are a treasured part. I was unaware then of how deeply significant those afternoon Bible studies, weekend overnight times, and Saturday outings were and how vividly they would remain to me. The seeds of encouragement, tender attention, prizing of God's Word, and godly advice took root and blossomed, resulting in friendship for a lifetime. The weekly hours were a "home-base" for my rapidly changing adolescent heart. Faithfulness and consistency ministered to me as much as wise teaching.

My years from 11 to 17 are filled with "Kodak moments"—our group of 25 to 30 singing "Pass It On" and other songs for Sunday night church . . . dressing up in our best to visit a nursing home, women's prison, or the county jail . . . pages of study notes filled out as we were taught from Proverbs, James, or even the Song of Solomon! There were private conversations with gentle reminders to free ourselves from bondage of cliques and pride . . . swimming, lunch, and study wrapped up in weekly summer days. There were beach trips in borrowed vans where we learned how to conduct ourselves in a hotel or nice restaurant. The investment did more than teach me the truths of Scripture. It taught me how to live. How grateful I am for the time spent amending the soil of my young heart.

—Melanie Beard Walker

Afterword

Afterword

It was the beginning of the 25th year of Bible study, a time of great excitement and celebration. So many trips, programs, and festivities were in the making. Then I heard the words, "You have breast cancer." Five surgeries and 6 months of chemotherapy lay before me. "Donna, you're going to be really tired," my surgeon told me. "You'll need a lot of help to keep the Bible studies going. You may even want to take a year off."

That was not even a consideration for me! I wrote a letter and sent it to all the girls involved in Bible study to explain what was going on and what lay before me. I wanted them to understand that we would need a tremendous group effort in order for Bible study to work that year. Everyone, from the brand-new 5th-graders all the way up to the seniors in high school, jumped right in. My staff held the organization of the ministry together but the girls ministered to each other. It was a beautiful thing to watch. Although I was present physically for most meetings, many times I felt too weak to actually teach.

Hundreds of girls who had grown up in Bible study came forward to lead high school groups, help chaperon trips, teach, or just spend time with the girls. I was overwhelmed as I sat back and observed the harvest. The investment I had made through the years was being returned in overflowing abundance.

After surviving that year of battling cancer, my oncologist approached me and said, "Is there any reason you have to live your life as if you were running a marathon every day? You are doing very well but your body has been highly assaulted." I would add to that, highly insulted!

After much prayer and many tears, I knew that I should completely give up the 5th-, 6th-, 7th-, and 8th-grade Bible study groups and continue with discipleship groups for 9th, 10th, 11th, and 12th grades. Again I wrote a letter to the hundreds of girls. I offered the lessons I had written to any teachers who wanted to step forward and lead a group. I promised to help them get started, be their coach, and then let go.

I wasn't prepared for what happened. I gave up 4 Bible study clubs and 12 sprang up in their place. I was amazed to watch high school seniors step forward and lead as well as teach the younger girls. They fully understood how to do it and needed no adult supervision, although a parent was always present in case of an emergency.

Several years ago, a guidance counselor from a public high school called me. "We've noticed that the girls who are part of your Bible study groups have the highest degree of leadership skills at the school," she said. And then she asked, "What do you teach them?" I had to think about it for a while because I had not begun Community Ministry for Girls and the Bible study groups in order to develop leaders. Yet leadership resulted among the girls who had been a part of the ministry. I sought to disciple. The discipleship reproduced leaders, all ages, all personalities, different situations. Even a 10-year-old girl can take what she has learned and share it with other children. Some girls are natural-born leaders while others lead in one small area. It doesn't matter. When you put it all together, it becomes a gift that keeps on giving.

Oh Donna, I wish you could be here. I miss you so much. I miss sitting around talking with you and our discipleship group. We had so much fun. I don't think that I ever really thanked you for everything you did for me. Donna, I don't think I would be where I am today if you hadn't been there to help me along. I don't know how you put up with me. I will have to admit I was pretty obnoxious. Thanks! Thanks for being such a great encouragement to me. I can't even begin to tell you how much that has meant to me.
        —from a college sophomore

Dear Donna,
How are you? It has been so long and I miss you so much. I also miss our Bible study. I was always so encouraged, uplifted, and on fire for Christ when I would leave Bible study with our group. There are lots of different groups to become involved in here but none like that. Thanks for that time and I wish it could last. I'll just pray for something like that.
        —from a college freshman

Dear Donna,
I can't even begin to tell you how much Bible study has meant to me the last 8 years. It was God through you who really taught me what it really means to be a Christian. You gave me the road map to follow which leads to Him. Your faith is a continuing encouragement to me. The wonderful ways God works in your life make me want to get to know Him more intimately. The foundation that you have helped me to set in Him is so strong and deep that I know I can't be moved next year. I hope and pray that I will be able to start a group that desires to go as deep as our discipleship went. No words can express my gratefulness to you for completely dedicating your life to us and teaching us to walk uprightly. I'm scared to think

where I might be right now if God had not placed you in my life. I will continue to pray for Bible study and will write you and tell you how I am holding up in college.
            —from a girl leaving for college

"Command those who are rich in this present world not to be arrogant nor to put their hope in wealth, which is so uncertain, but to put their hope in God, who richly provides us with everything for our enjoyment. Command them to do good, to be rich in good deeds, and to be generous and willing to share. In this way they will lay up treasure for themselves as a firm foundation for the coming age, so that they may take hold of the life that is truly life. . . . Guard what has been entrusted to your care" (1 Tim. 6:17–20).

Appendix

Appendix

Community Ministry for Girls Bible Study: A Year at a Glance

"And Jesus grew in wisdom and stature, and in favor with God and men" (Luke 2:52).

This verse is the basis for Community Ministry for Girls Bible Study. I want the girls to grow mentally, physically, spiritually, and socially—to be well-balanced Christians. Community Ministry for Girls encompasses all of these areas.

While you must form a club that meets the needs and desires of the girls with whom you will work, an overview of our schedule may be helpful to you. We begin Bible studies each fall on the Monday after Labor Day. This allows ample time for the girls to adjust to their school schedules before adding afternoon activities. We meet throughout the school year and end the third week of May. Girls may start in a club when they are in the 5th grade and continue until they graduate from high school. The following summary profiles each group.

Fifth Grade

When: Thursdays, 3:00–4:30 P.M.

Where: At girls' homes

What We Do: Sing, have refreshments, have Bible study, divide into small groups to pray, learn Bible verses, play games

Small-Group Leaders: High school girls

What We Study: How to deal with cliques, the Book of James, and the Book of 1 John

How We Reach Out: Service projects involving nursing home visits for Halloween, Christmas, Valentine's Day, and Easter; Christmas caroling for food to give to the needy

How We Play: Bible Study Olympics, lock-ins, swimming parties

Sixth Grade

When: Tuesdays, 3:00–4:30 P.M.

Where: At girls' homes

What We Do: Sing, have refreshments, have Bible study, divide into small groups to pray, learn Bible verses, play games

Small-Group Leaders: High school girls

What We Study: Proverbs 31, The Godly Woman. We focus on a different characteristic each week. We also study a series of topics that show the girls how to live the Christian life.

How We Reach Out: Service projects involving nursing home visits for Halloween, Christmas, Valentine's Day, and Easter; Christmas caroling for food to give to the needy

How We Play: Bible Study Olympics, lock-ins, swimming parties

Seventh Grade
When: Mondays, 3:00-4:30 P.M.; or Fridays, 6:45–7:45 A.M.
Where: At girl's homes close to the school
What We Do: Sing, have refreshments, have Bible study, learn Bible verses, divide into small groups with high school leaders
What We Study: The Sermon on the Mount and other topics for Christian living
How We Reach Out: Service projects at Halloween, Christmas, Valentine's Day, and Easter; Christmas caroling for food to give to the needy
How We Play: The girls take turns going to dinner with their leaders each week. Those who memorize 50 Scripture verses during the year are rewarded with a trip to Atlanta. We also take weekend trips to the lake and have swimming parties and lock-ins.

Eighth Grade
When: Wednesdays, 3:00–4:30 P.M.
Where: At girls' homes close to the school
What We Do: Have refreshments, sing, have Bible study, learn Bible verses
Small-Group Leaders: High school seniors lead closing time each week.
What We Study: The Book of 1 Thessalonians
How We Reach Out: Service projects at a home for abused women and children; writing cards and letters to younger girls; collecting food for the needy
How We Play: Dinner with leaders, weekend trips to the lake and the beach, trip to Atlanta, spend-the-night parties

Ninth-Grade Discipleship
When: Tuesdays, 5:00–6:30 P.M.
Where: Apartment club house or meeting room
What We Do: Sing praise choruses, learn Bible verses, have Bible study and prayer/share time
Group Leaders: Girls in and just out of college
What We Study: Various topical Bible studies
How We Reach Out: Ministering at Hope Lodge for the American Cancer Society, serving as big sisters to girls in various Bible studies across the country (email, pen pals), meeting other needs through ministry

Discipleship for High School Sophomores, Juniors, and Seniors
Most girls in Community Ministry for Girls Bible studies have by now been involved for 5 years. They must make a real commitment to continue during their high school years. Our high school discipleship groups meet on a weeknight for about an hour and a half. Girls are involved in two major service projects:

Hope Lodge is a facility where cancer patients and their caretakers may stay free of charge while the patients undergo treatments. The girls visit people staying at this facility by grade one night a month. The girls love it and so do the patients. They make posters for each patient with Bible verses and colorful decorations and tape these to each person's door. They host theme nights for the residents, such as Make Your Own Sundae, Hawaiian Luau, and Valentine's Day, as well as other seasonal activities like dyeing Easter eggs. They visit with patients one-on-one and get to know them so that they will know better how to pray for them. The girls often bring their guitars and sing with patients and their caretakers.

Relay for Life is a fund-raiser for the American Cancer Society. High schoolers in Community Ministry for Girls divide into four teams, one for each grade, to participate in this event by walking and running. Collectively, they have raised over $80,000 to date to aid in the fight against cancer.

In addition to these two service projects, the girls have responded throughout the years to many other needs that have arisen. They have collected clothes for hurricane and tornado victims, medical supplies for earthquake victims, and books for an orphanage. They held a fun run and raised over $3,000 for a home for abused women and children. They have showered sick children with cards and toys.

A huge part of discipleship at this stage in the girls' lives is helping them develop strong friendships, which in turn will help them stand against negative peer pressure. To foster this, we take a lot of trips on weekends and in the summer to lakes and beaches and to the mountains to hike. The older girls sometimes even have the opportunity to go on cruises and trips to cities like New York.

Discipleship lessons for high school girls include how to know God's plan for your life, how to have an effective quiet time, and apologetics. But lessons must always fit the group and their needs. For example, a young woman who had been a member of a Bible study group as a teenager recently started a club in the state where she now lives. As a schoolteacher, she noticed how unkind the girls were to each other. She spoke with her principal and told her about her experiences with Community Ministry for Girls. She asked if it would be possible for her to begin a Bible study club for 6th-grade girls at the school after school. She sent letters to parents explaining the fact that this would be a Christian club. Over 20 girls are now a part of the group. The mentor for these girls had to start with the very basics since most of the students had never even been to church.

While our experience has been to have Bible study clubs during the school year, clubs can continue all year long or just during the summer. One leader started a group for inner-city girls just for the summer. She found that most of the girls were around with nothing to do. Their Bible study club met several times a week throughout the summer. The leader is the key to success for any group. An investment of even a couple of months can change the course of girls' lives.

> *"Those who are wise will shine like the brightness of the heavens, and those who lead many to righteousness, like the stars for ever and ever"* (Dan. 12:3).

Anita puts it this way: "When I was about to start 7th grade, I asked a friend of mine who was 25 years old to start a 'club' for my friends and me. We wanted to learn about makeup, hair, modeling, and also more about the Bible and what God had to say to young girls. Donna agreed to teach us and we quickly grew to 60 girls, meeting once a week. Although going to different schools, we continued to meet together weekly through our senior year of high school. Through studying God's Word, service projects, and simply hanging out together, we learned how to have deep friendships, how to deal with peer pressure and conflicts, how to reach out, and how to apply God's Word to our daily lives. It also prepared us for college and the pressures we would face there. I can't begin to tell you what an incredible impact it had on my life."

The world is changed one life at a time. God speaks. We obey. He shows us more; and as we become obedient to that, He shows us even more. This continues throughout our lifetime. Only disobedience can counteract this progression.

Anita and her husband, Billy, are now in Scottsdale, Arizona, planting a church. Francie, their daughter, is now the age of girls who began Community Ministry for Girls in Birmingham. Anita asked if I would come to Scottsdale to share with those young girls and their mothers about the concept and benefits of Bible study. In her letter of invitation Anita said, "It has been my desire that when my own little girl was in 5th grade, she too could be a part of something like this. With this in mind, we have invited your daughters to an ice-cream party where Donna will get them excited about the Bible study. We would also like to invite you to a luncheon where she will give us a vision for it as well. I hope you can come and that your girls will be a part of something that I believe will be life-changing." Over 90 girls poured into Anita's home that day with Francie greeting each one who walked through the door. Anita played the guitar, all sang, and another generation of Bible study girls was born—completely across the country.

> *"The desert and the parched land will be glad; the wilderness will rejoice and blossom. . . . The burning sand will become a pool, the thirsty ground bubbling springs" (Isa. 35:1,7).*

The world is changed one life at a time. And that gift goes on and on.

Also by
Donna
Margaret
Greene

1-56309-756-7

Available in Spring 2003 in Christian bookstores everywhere.